chapter 1

THE VALUE OF DREAMS

Do we live in the same world, where our feet are always on the ground? Or are we living in another world, a world of thought or dream? Which one is true? Which is real? Who are you? What brought you here? Where did you come from? What are your plans for the future?

You will discover more by reflecting on and working hard on your dreams. The yogic approach is to dreaming to reach the Divine within. This is what the Eastern teachings refer to as the Guru (spiritual teacher), or the Higher Self. Jesus calls it the kingdom of God within[2].

Yogaic methods of working with dreams stress independence and a deeper understanding of ourselves as individuals. We create our dreams and learn from them our personal language of unconscious. It is very joyous to make our own discoveries. This gives us the strength and courage to continue. We gain self-confidence by finding the answers within. Our aches and pains can be seen in many different ways so we don't have to rely on others. Because we all have our own symbol language, there can't be generalizations about symbols.

It is possible to look at our own lives and see how we have learned to use language. It is important to not assume that the learning process that began as a child has ended. As we learn more, our skills are refined and expanded. Our tools are more effective when we learn how to use them. You may be surprised at how your words are used.

If we allow our unconscious to speak, it will give us a lot of information. We need to be careful because we don't know what our unconscious is saying. We have evolved into amazing acrobats in our conscious minds. Everything can be argued and rationalized. The unconscious knocks at the door and says "Look, I'm there.".

Remember me." It is important to recognize the unconscious's efforts to draw our attention. "Please listen to my voice." If we don't, we can find ourselves in a difficult or even traumatic situation in our lives.

Strangely, though we may think we know each others and think we know ourselves well, when it comes down to the language of our unconscious, we are actually quite ignorant. It is important to learn it like a foreign language.

Ask yourself: "Do I want study my symbolism?" Are you really interested in yourself? What are your goals? What are you hoping to achieve? This questions creates curiosity and motivates you to set goals.

A well-known tale tells of a little girl who walks along a road and comes to a crossroads. She wonders if this is the right direction for her. I don't know." She continues to look but is unable to make a decision. She suddenly sees a hut. An old witch appears and knocks at the door.

The little girl wants to know which way is best.

The witch replies by asking "What's your destination?"

The little girl replies, "I don't know."

The witch says, "Then it doesn't matter what road you take.".

Tell the witch in your subconscious where you want to go. Once you have defined your ideals and figured out what type of person you want, your dreams will help you get there. Dreams can help you determine the next step and how to get there. Your unconscious will guide you, but you must follow the guidance and act accordingly.

One young woman who lived at the Ashram[3] claimed that her spiritual teacher appeared in dreams to tell her that she should stay there. He gave her clear instructions to follow. One day, she met a young man who gave her specific instructions. She was suddenly able to have a series of completely new dreams. His message was: "This is your man." Follow him."

I asked: "Which dreams are you most certain are true?" What was your first dream? At the time, you believed they were higher guidance. But now, you tell me your new dreams are sending you a different message.

Did the unconscious play tricks on her? I don't think so. I think not.

Her spiritual potential was revealed to her. By ignoring her previous dreams, she chose to ignore her spiritual potential and interpret the new messages in a manner that satisfied her emotional needs. In this instance, the man was only with her for a year before she left. Our potential will be revealed by our unconscious. If we don't follow through and use it, the unconscious will show us what is next best. This is often the most common way of living.

Your Divine birthright is yours, but you are responsible for not claiming it. It is impossible to say you were not given the chance. Until you put more effort into your growth, you are exactly where you need to be. Your goal can be the Divine within. You can find out if there are any underlying principles, but you must be determined to discover them for your own good.

Dreams can help you stay motivated and nourished. They can also be a positive outlet to self-interest and self expression. It is possible to use our inherent selfishness in a positive way: to get to know ourselves. The many images you see in your dreams can give you both positive information and negative information about yourself and the stage of your development. You can learn from your dreams what no one else can. You can get twenty different opinions on yourself from 20 people, so what does that mean for you? How can you tell if someone is trying to help you develop? How do you determine if someone is being used as a Divine channel or not? Through a dream, your guru will tell you: "Look. You must do one thing. Dreams will help you get rid of criticism and judgment. If you're open to listening, they can have a profound effect on your life and change your outlook.

Your mind is too busy during the day to hear the inner guru. To justify your actions and to coax or coerce others into following you, mental gymnastics is what you do. Emotions drive you to action, so you can't be free. The busy mind goes to sleep and the higher thoughts that can help you deal with your problems, such as the pains and aches of your body, fade away. We are unable to see things when we become too busy or too drawn by the bright colors and brightness of life.

It is common to say that we want to become a channel for something better. However, it is important to keep the channel clean. It's like opening an old water faucet and seeing all the dirt, rust, and silt. Dreams can be a wonderful way to show us dirt in our water pipes and to help us identify it. Although some things might not be obvious, dreams can help us identify them. This invaluable guidance will always be within us.

We pride ourselves on our intellect and logic, but we also create the most absurd problems in our own lives. This is what the unconscious tells us in a slow, gentle, kind way. It gives us the message step by step so we don't get overwhelmed by our little ego. In a loving and beautiful way, dreams can help us to be more aware. Sometimes, they can also shock or shake us awake. But only when we don't listen or we don't want to hear the message.

To understand dreams we must see their material. What is their fabric? It can be very fine or very gross. Or it could even be very beautiful. The unconscious receives its message from those situations that are most open to it in our waking states.

We can learn so much about ourselves by looking at our dreams and keeping detailed records. This is a good place to start. We may also receive instructions from our dreams later. Eventually, we may be able to open up to Higher Consciousness.

Once you have erected your tabernacle, your secret place of worship, then you can begin Jacob's Ladder or the steps required to reach the Higher Self from the good foundation. Once you are able to sense intuition and finer feelings, it is time to start building Jacob's Ladder. You need not rush and stomp on everything. The first thing you do is notice the change and then ask "What does it mean?"?
"Why did this sudden occur to me?"

You should first learn how to work with dreams using the method that I will show you: write down your dreams, analyze them, make your dream symbol dictionary, then look into how your subconscious uses symbols and words to communicate messages. A whole new world can be opened up by studying your dreams and expanding your knowledge of symbolism, imagery, and the psychology of your subconscious.

It is like being able to recognize the Most High within yourself. Listening to your dreams can help you discover the Cathedral of Consciousness in which you were born. Your dream voice will direct you: "Come along. This door is open. You will find another room that you can access. Continue down the hall. There are two more doors. You will be able to see the light next time.

chapter 2

THE METHOD

This method of exploring dreams is safe and secure. It will provide clear results in a short time. Because dreams can be confusing at first, it will take some time. Your Higher Self will not reveal the truth of the unconscious language until you are able to speak it. As you understand the process of understanding your dreams and gain strength and the willingness to face the challenges they present, your dreams will become clearer.

The unconscious is extremely kind. The unconscious does not come in and tell you, "You are a bad person!" You can change that! The unconscious is gracious and will give you the information in the most appropriate way. Sometimes it will be very direct and sometimes in a very cultural manner. The unconscious will be your most trusted, loyal and trustworthy teacher. You will be able to speak of the God or the Guru within one day. It won't be fiction or theory anymore.

What are your options for working with dreams?

RECALL

The first step is to accurately recall your dreams. First, create a strong desire to recall your dreams.

Before you fall asleep, address yourself with your first name. Then, make the suggestion that you remember your dream as soon as possible. This suggestion will help you to remember your dream twice.

Be sure to have everything you need next to your bed, including a pencil, paper, and a flashlight. On top of your paper, write the word "Dream" and the date along with the day, month, and year. If you have a tape recorder, make sure the tape is in place and ready to go. You can train yourself to not set an alarm or lower the volume if it is.

Write down your dreams immediately after you wake up in the morning.

You can't remember a dream but you have to take action. Before you get out of bed, write down what you feel or think about the day. This means that you must resist the temptation to let your lazy mind take control. You will find that your mind is very capable of obedience if you insist on it. This is your first thought. It shows how intense you are demanding of yourself. Write down your thoughts and feelings if you think, "Oh, it didn't seem like I had a dream." It may be helpful to record the fact that you don't feel good about the dream.

If you don't remember a dream after three weeks, you need to be honest with yourself. Sometimes, we have to close the blinds in order to see something that we don't want.

DREAM RECORD

Even if your dream is very brief, it is important to write it down. These details are very important. You must be honest with yourself and not change your appearance to look better. If you alter the dream, you will not reap the benefits. To ensure that your record is accurate, sign your name.

To ensure that the main content is clear, you must first write it down. Next, add details. For example, the staircase could have been on the left or right side of the house. You can add all details to the beginning of the story without losing the overall view. Even if you only remember a few snippets from your dreams, it is worth writing them down in any circumstance. You will recall many more details if you are willing to remember them.

Write down your dream as accurately as possible if it is a nightmare you don't want to remember. It is worth reading it at least three to four times. It is worth thinking about. It is important to take the time to think it through. Once you are done, it is time to destroy it. It is important to not ignore it. No matter what the dream says, you must face it. Otherwise you will have a lot of skeletons hidden in your head. You may find it comforting to know that you might see something completely different from the symbolism or dream later on, once you have gained acceptance and understanding.

COMMENTARY

Next, make a quick comment: What did you feel when your body woke up?

Anxious, overjoyed, elated, miserable, fearful, worried, startled, indifferent? It may be a brief description or a single line. It may be a crucial clue.

Was your heart beating fast? Did you feel anxious? Did you make a fist of it? Did you hold your hand tight over your face? Did you reach for something, like a watch, on the night table? What is the best way to sleep? On your left? To your right? Your back? On your stomach?

When you get up, write down your emotions. You can easily change the color of your feelings later if you try to recreate them. You might feel a fear when you wake up from a dream about mountains. Later, you may find that the mountains were a symbol for aspiration and that it made you feel good. Memory is not reliable.

The degree of intensity of a dream--indicated by your feelings when you wake up and by your immediate inter-pretation--gives you a clue about the dream's importance.

INITIAL INTERPRETATION

What is your first, or most inspired interpretation of the dream? Even if the interpretation seems insufficient, write it down. Even if you think you don't know what it means, . . It's quite confused," this is at most part what the dream refers to--confusion. Next, dig into the details to discover the cause of the confusion. You will find the precise answer in your dream.

This dream was shared by a friend who is an engineer:

Bridges Over Roofs

It was a beautiful beach on a river. Instead of beautiful landscapes, where there should have been gardens, flowers and trees, there was an industrial area. The engineer was building a bridge across the river to one house's roof and another house's roof. There were many steps on the bridge that were very unusual. One was very steep, and then another was very curvy, with many steps going down, and then the next going upward.

He told me that he didn't believe in my dream.

I asked him: "If you were given this project by someone, what would you tell them as engineers?"

“Confused nonsense.”
"What is it about your life that deserves the same description?"

Although the dream was not itself confused, he clearly stated to him that his current plans were arising out of confusion and would result in nonsensical outcomes.

CONSCIOUS CONCERNS

Write a comment about what led to your dream. Keep a daily journal and refer to the previous day's events and thoughts. What was going through your head? These could be thoughts, fears, or actions. Note the details: My father in law visited. My boss called me to his office. My religion is Protestant. I entered a Catholic church to take a few minutes for me. I sat down and recited the rosary. My eyes were drawn to the title of the book three times.

Perhaps you had a bad day. Maybe you wanted to sign a contract but it didn't happen, or you applied for a job and was unsuccessful, or maybe you just had a hard time getting hired.

Disagreement with a loved-one. Maybe there was something small but that stayed with your thoughts, like a melody that echoed through your head all day. These lasting impressions should be recorded. These impressions are vital. To determine if your dreams are affected by them, you should include any information that might be affecting your dreams, such as your food intake, atmospheric pressure, or phase of the moon. Noting any influences before bed, such as TV, movies, books, or last-minute conversations, is a good idea. [4]

Also, consider the underlying issues that are affecting your life. Are you pursuing any specific goals? Do you need to make a decision? It is important to be open with your investigations. You have to be open about what is happening in your everyday life that might contribute to your dream?

KEY WORDS/SYMBOLS

Note the "key words", which are the most important words (including people and objects), in the order they appear in your dream. This will allow you to determine the exact interpretation. This is a methodical approach but will work.

Write down the meaning of the words, not as it would appear in a dictionary. But what does the word mean to you? Even if the meaning is irrelevant to the dream.

[5]

What does a car refer to? A tree, a flower or a key? What does running refer to? Running can be defined as driving, jumping, closing, opening, or stopping. Sometimes, you might choose a set of words and other times a single word. It is a good idea to look at a key phrase as both a whole and individual words. The meaning will be clearer if you do this.

Let's say that you have a dream that you are driving down the highway. Imagine that you go into a house and open a window to see outside. You can see an animal or a bear. What does a highway actually mean? What does walking mean to you? What does it mean to walk into a house? What does it mean to walk into a house? Are there any other details you can recall about the dream? How was the house? Small, large, light, dark, or big? What was the location of the window? Are there curtains on the window? There were no curtains. The window was opened. How did you open that window? You can only remember what you saw in your dream. Perhaps you saw the window opening by itself. You might find a window suddenly opening. What does the window signify? What does looking out look like? What does it mean to look out for a bear? Did you see any trees, bushes, flowers, or was it all bare? Bear among the trees. What does it mean to be a tree? What type of trees are they? Are they still alive? Snow-covered? Cherry trees? Apple trees with blossoms Did the bear run towards you or just stare at you?

I was looking out of the window. I. What did you think of yourself as I? Which is it? The window. The window. It's transparent and keeps out the rain, snow, and cold. Is it the window to the mind? Ah! Ah! You were looking out of the window. Looking out. Looking out. As you gain understanding, each symbol will become more complex. It will be easy to see the truth behind what may seem absurd or unreal.

INTERPRETATION

You can now interpret your dream using the information you have gathered by opening the symbols. Start by going through your dream key word-by-keyword, then in groups and then in complete sentences. Finally, you can begin to piece together the message.

You can see your dream from many angles. Sometimes a single dream can be seen from multiple perspectives. How does the rest of your dream look if you place the emphasis on one thing? How does the rest look if you place emphasis on one part of the dream? Next, take a look at the entire dream. It's like interior design. "What if I put my dining room furniture there, and my living room furniture here? And the TV in the hall?" This will give you an idea of how it looks. However, you will find out after you have tried it.

It is important to go through this process.

APPLICATION

It is not enough to interpret your dreams and get their messages. Your evolution will only be accelerated if you take action on the messages. How can you expect to see any results if you don't act on the information you find? Intellectualizing doesn't take you anywhere. Your understanding must be applied in your daily life.

WORKING IN GROUPS

The dream provides all the information you need to work independently. But, other people can help you to dig deeper into your investigation by asking questions. That is why it is helpful to work with a group.

You will discover that everyone has a different language of the unconscious when you work in a group. They can easily see the differences between husband and wife if they come together in the same group. They will also be able to talk about their dreams and realize how significant their differences can sometimes be. Do they want to be friends despite their differences? Are they willing to let their differences be a part of each other's growth? While insisting on your way can hinder growth, listening and accepting can help you to grow. Great trust and confidence can be achieved when people work together to realize their dreams.

Bring a dream you've worked on to your dream group. The group can help you explore other possibilities if you interpret your dream first. You will feel happy if you share your dream with me without first interpreting it. It may be difficult to accept. Even if you accept it temporarily, I cannot interpret your dream as if I were dreaming. I would receive a completely different message.

If you've already dreamed your dream, you can ask the group, "Could it be this?" and "Have they looked at that?" or "From what I have gotten from you, I think the dream could be meaning. . "There is always something to be learned from different perspectives, and sometimes you might miss the point. For example, the woman who believed she had evidence that her mother was a horrible woman but in reality, her dream was revealing her own traits.

Consider other perspectives, but don't depend on them. You may not like what you see, but another person might be more objective. It is possible that it is not always so. You can accept or reject an interpretation of another person's view, but it is up to your discretion. Other people can help you see things through another lens. They cannot force you to see it because you are an individual. The group members can offer you a different perspective. You must first interpret your dream. Otherwise, you could become dependent.

You can do your work alone, but be clear about what you are trying to accomplish when you meet up as a team. It is not a time for a social gathering. You only have so much time. Nobody knows. This is something you should consider.

Do it now and not later.

Be aware of your thoughts, feelings, and motivations when you're in the group. If you are only looking to please people, don't pretend you want to share your dreams. You must be honest with yourself as well as with others.

SUMMARY OF METHOD

- *Dream record*: Write your dream quickly and honestly.
- *Signature: Add the date and your signature below. Commentary: Fill in*
- *any missing details. Describe your emotions.*

- *Initial interpretation*: What is your immediate impression of he dream's meaning?
- *Conscious concerns*: Briefly note events that could have led to the dream.
- *Key words/symbols*: Select the main words from the dream and write down associations and meanings to you.
- *Interpretation*: See how the symbolic meanings fit together to give messages on several levels.
- *Application*: Apply the dream's message to your life.
- *Dream group: You can join others to gain different perspectives if you find it useful.*

chapter 3

AN EXAMPLE

Here's an example of a student's dream, first with his interpretation, then with my questions.

The Basement (a student's dream record)

An elderly, gray-haired, motherless woman is found in the basement. Her husband has silently left her. She is completely alone, though he gives her plenty of money. We descend in an elevator that then runs horizontally through open basements and out into the country.

(signature of dreamer)

COMMENTARY

After the dream, I felt some compassion for the woman but it was very mild.

CONSCIOUS CONCERNS

Just completed the three-month course in the Ashram. [6] I am trying to overcome unknown obstacles that hinder my growth, so that I can take the next step.

INITIAL INTERPRETATION

A change in attitude is something that can be achieved.

KEY WORDS

Basement--is vital area, storage area, and a packing area--warmth. enthusiasm. heat. consuming corner.--backed into. not comfortable. out of the swim. the woman- intuitive. receptive. nurturing. stoic. staying power. emotional mother- -warm, philosophical. productive. selfless. compassionate husband- reluctant companion. independent. energy source money.-energy, resource, freedom elevator.--to switch levels. mechanical. no effort. -level buildings.

Country--natural, without social implications, changes

THE DREAMER'S INTERPRETATION

With some maturity and deeper insight, my intuitive parts are now more mature. My active side provides energy but no support. My mechanical abilities are working at a lower level than I expected, thanks to foundations and structures that need completion.

HOW TO EXPAND THE INTERPRETATION

We can see that the dream is not like every other house. However, this one has one. Could this be a symbol of the unconscious? The dreamer is trying to protect himself. He doesn't say "I am in basement sitting by an open fire." He says "In basement sitting by an open fire is a. . "Using the third person to describe the character seated there. He must look at the basement to see which part of him is there. He can say the following to help him see that the old lady is relating to himself: "I am in basement, sitting at an empty fire," or "In basement, I am sitting at an empty fire." This immediately puts it in perspective: "That's the place where a part me is--in the vital area, the storage area, the deeper level. Some part of me is in touch with the unconscious.

A fire can't be considered "empty". There must either be a fire or it isn't. Even a pile of glowing embers does not mean that it is empty. If the fire has gone out, it is not lit. An "empty fire" should have a particular meaning.

Asking yourself questions is part of understanding a dream's meaning. The dreamer may ask, "Is it really in the fire? Or is it in my perception of it?" Does my perception of the fire seem empty? The dreamer thought the empty fire represented a lack of enthusiasm. But could it be more? "Here, I am in basement. Here is the fire. What's the next step? The dreamer may have many opinions and misconceptions about life, as well as the purpose of living. He may also have many past experiences, some of which have not been addressed. It is better to burn them than keep them around. It's like holding stock in a company that is no longer relevant. Better to dispose of them than clutter up the basement. This is just one option.

Another aspect is that the fire, if it is not lit, is waiting for something else to light it. It is also waiting to burn away old ideas and lack of understanding of the purpose of living. This is similar to the fire in alchemy, where metal is transformed into precious metals and dross is melted away. Fire is a symbol of wisdom and the destruction of ignorance in Eastern symbolism.

Yes, the dreamer can inspire more enthusiasm. The symbolism refers to all of these aspects simultaneously. He says that fire is warmth, and that enthusiasm, heat, and consuming are the three aspects of the dream. Perhaps he's dreaming that he must go into his basement to clean out all the corners. He can see the basement by lighting a fire. The dream could be a reminder to us all that we must see the unconscious and do our best to deal with it.

An old, gray-haired woman is in the corner. She may be someone's mother. The dreamer said, "The corner: backed in, not comfortable, out the swim." The woman: intuitive, open, nurturing, caring, stoic and emotional

Dreamers are more concerned with keeping their intuitive, receptive side of themselves in an uncomfortable place than making it a part his life. She is alone. He might ask, "How can I cut off my intuition, receptivity nurturing qualities, emotions?" He might need to reflect on his relationship with his mother or his spiritual mother or guru. Is the dream a reflection of his relationship with either mother or guru?

You can ask yourself what image you have in your head when you think of an "old gray-haired lady." Does he deny the aging process? What does it mean for death? Is age wisdom gained through experience or the soul?

> The dreamer in this instance is a man. However, the gray-haired old woman is the dreamer

His soul could be symbolised by this. This would indicate that his inner wisdom, or Light, has been neglected and not recognized. The dream shows that "the husband," which could refer to how the dreamer views himself, active, independent, and a resource of energy, has quietly left her. Perhaps he became so interested in life, business success, and the outer world. It indicates that nothing significant has occurred. He ignored her and left quietly, rather than paying attention to his soul. Although he may eat a healthy diet, he doesn't nourish his soul. He sends her only enough energy to keep her alive.

The first marriage spiritually is between the males and females within, the union or reason and intuition. [7] The dreamer's female side is left behind, while the man's part lives and pursues his passions elsewhere. He sends money and energy frequently (out of obligation). guilt? He is telling me, "Don't bother me." Because if I bother you, I will have to examine myself and ask: "Who am I?" Why am I here? Why was I created? What is the point of me going into the basement? What are you doing in that corner? Why do you think I must recognize that you are part of me and I am part you? He is giving enough to not be bothered. This could be an indication that he believes he can do enough to make up for a feeling of guilt or heartlessness?

Dreamers will eventually need to accept the feminine part of themselves. When he does, he'll be able to access the wisdom and knowledge that is the Divine feminine.

Next, he will descend in an elevator. Are you familiar with what happens when you enter an elevator? The elevator will take you up or down depending on your destination. You must make sure that you press the right button to ensure the elevator moves up or down to your destination. This elevator is very peculiar. It moves horizontally, then it descends. This could be a symbol of a linear thinking style. Instead of traveling up and down to different levels, the elevator travels along the same level. Our Western way of thinking is rational and linear. This is a result of our influence on Aristotle and Greek thought. The horizontal elevator confirms linear thinking and shows that the dreamer may not be in touch with his full potential. Maybe he's only understanding superficially.

Perhaps the dreamer has misperceptions about the spiritual life.

Thinking that higher values require sacrifice and martyrdom to seek them out is absurd. This is a complete nonsense. In that case, there would be very few people willing to take your place. We need people who are willing to live in the world but also seek higher values. It doesn't matter how many austerities or robes that you have, if you don't live your ideals and help other people live them in a practical manner, then it is just theory. Doctrines create barriers. They can be used to divide people from different religions. It is not the application of higher values and awareness that matters. This is what makes someone spiritual.

Other basements are also open so I suspect the dreamer is in touch with others who have been brave enough to look into their unconscious. Perhaps the elevator will lead the dreamer to new horizons. Life takes on new meaning when you see the possibilities in your life. Even if there's no enthusiasm initially and no apparent purpose, it can be a source of joy. You will find your purpose. The dream is a clear message.

What appears to be a small dream with only a few lines can actually contain a huge message if you look closely. This is a beautiful dream.

chapter 4

SYMBOLS

The dreaming mind transforms our everyday experiences into metaphors and symbols. It combines many ideas into one image. It's as if the unconscious takes all of our everyday experiences and creates something new. We give it a name: a rope. A rope is only as long as the strands are connected. What happens to the rope if it is taken apart? We discover the fibers and strands that connect us to each other in rich, multilayered ways as we "disassemble" our dreams through exploring the symbols.

What is it that we dream in metaphors and symbols? Everything is related to what we have experienced in the past. Most people see the world through their eyes. Our minds are constantly creating images. It is how the mind thinks and is stimulated by emotions and imagination. It's also how memory works. These images are used by the unconscious to communicate its symbolic messages.

Because you are a unique person and have different life experiences, your dream symbols may have a different meaning than others. Although there may be similarities in their meanings, they will not be identical. Just as there aren't two identical leaves on the same tree, so there won't be any. It is important to recognize our uniqueness and importance, but not in an egotistical way. This healthy sense of self-importance is essential for the ability to continue exploring ourselves and to find the way to self-knowledge.

What symbols are in your dreams and how can you approach them?

PEOPLE IN YOUR DREAMS

Consider the characters in your dreams first as part of you--what I refer to as "personality aspects". Each of us has many personalities that can move into the forefront in different situations. Every personality aspect also has its own ego. [8] This perspective allows you to see the traits of the characters in your dreams as being part of yourself. You can overcome your own weaknesses if you are able to accept the criticisms that dreams bring you through the characters.

The unconscious is extremely compassionate. Your unconscious doesn't say "You are this or that." It says "Look, this person is not for you." Are you wondering why you don't like her? These are the reasons. You might find these characteristics in yourself if you take a look at your own life. It would be a good idea to imagine your despotic father or your crabby little brother. What will you do about your bad temper? The mirror in your dream will show you exactly who you are.

Your positive qualities and potential through inspiring characters may be reflected in the dream. It could be that the message is, "Look, you are not only your mistakes." This is your kindness, generosity and humor. While you might not possess all of the same characteristics as this person, you may have some. This will allow you to see the interconnectedness of all beings, and realize that you are not an isolated island.

In your dreams, you might see crowds. How do you relate to crowds? Are you aware of where your place is? Do you allow these crowds to manipulate you or are you aware of your own individuality and take responsibility for your actions? Our lives are influenced by the power of other minds. Our world is home to billions of minds. There are thousands, if not millions of them in our city. We live among hundreds of people and our families, as well as those around us. It is important to understand how these influences affect our lives. These influences can be reflected in dreams.

The I within dreams is what makes them unique. Who is this I? Who is looking and who is acting? There are many I's. What do you mean when you say "I see", or "I think" or "I live in a cave?" Which personality aspect do I belong to? What do I mean? This is the first step in clarifying the I. Where is the I? Who or what is it that says "I"? Who knows what I am?

I drive. Who is the I who drives? Who has the final say? What drives you?

I am stopped. What's the I now? Someone is stopping. It's someone else who stops you. Who is that authority who can use its power to make you stop?

I'm worried. Who am I at this moment? What is it that worries you and who is it?

I do make a very quiet connection. This is a new I. I do, act, make, and I am the doer. What happens when there's silence? What's the connection?

I am aware. Another I. The I of recognition. The I of recognition.

This is the way I'm going. Who is the I who wants to follow its own path? Which is your way?

The I's in your dream can be viewed as aspects of your personality. Find out who they are, and how they behave. Sometimes, the I may have two meanings. One individual had an interesting dream which we only understood when the word eye (sense organ), was translated for me (me) by our eyes. The dream suddenly became crystal clear. I have a feeling that the unconscious uses words in this way to communicate with us. Old English used the expression "the eye in a wall" to refer to a window. The wall's opening can be seen by the eye. Any obstacle can be penetrated by the inner eye of wisdom. This human house will be flooded with knowledge. Which is my inner vision?

What will the ego look like in the dream? It may be a character that is too big or fat. Decide what to cut from this extravagant ego.

Once you understand the characters in your dream as part of you, you can then ask if they are also the actual people involved. If, for example, you see people trying to stop you from achieving your goal in your dream, this could be a sign of your personality. Let's have some fun. If you're different, they feel threatened. They feel justified in their laziness if they keep you from pursuing your goal.

Dreams can refer to your relationship with another person. Other dreams may be premonitions or warnings about someone. But, remember to always view your dreams as a personal reflection. Don't jump to conclusions too fast.

ANIMALS IN YOUR DREAMS

Human beings often don't recognize their connection to other forms of life. In our dreams, we might find many animal symbols. Animal symbolism was a common feature of ancient religions. This can sometimes be interpreted as indicating that people worshiped animals. They did. They recognized the animal's unique sharpness and power, and used symbols to communicate that power. The same goes for demons, gods, goddesses, and demons. A dream of Jesus can manifest as energy, but it could also manifest as a monster or a murderer. Each of us has a polarity, both the positive and negative. We are capable of expressing either. Although energy is one, how we use it can be a huge responsibility. How can you use this power that is truly one?

That is a good thing.

If you see animals in your dreams, ask yourself "What is the characteristic?" This will help you to identify a message that is important to you. It could be a sign that you need to strengthen or that you need to control. You may have a strength or an ability that is not fully recognized by the animal.

It is important to understand the meaning of each animal to you. A rat could be a sign that someone is trying to undermine you or your family. Another person may be reminded by a female rat that she is the most caring and affectionate mother. A dog can be interpreted as faithfulness and loyalty by one person, but aggressiveness and unpredictability to another. A dog may be associated with no pride by another person.

One dreamed of a large animal, but was not afraid to be attacked by it because it had downcast eyes. Someone was implying something: downcast eyes make it difficult to see the big picture clearly. The problem was sexual self-gratification. Because of the conditioning that made it look so sinful, the dream said, "There's no need to fear attack. But there's something that needs to been looked at clearly."

Every person has had experiences. These experiences are part of our lives and can help us interpret our dreams. Because each individual is different and has his or her own conditioning, there are no universal rules to understanding the symbol.

VEHICLES IN YOUR DREAMS

The car is our vehicle. I move using the vehicle that is my mind, my intellect, my thinking, reasoning. What is the vehicle of consciousness? Depending on the culture, the mind was represented by the horse, the camel, or the elephant in old fairy tales. The horse is as sacred in Europe as the cow in India. The mythical legends tell of a great knight riding his horse, which was his victory vehicle, into Valhalla, the heaven of ancient Norse gods. Modern times, however, the vehicle can be a car, a train or an airplane.

Take a look at the cars in your dreams. What vehicles do you see? Which vehicle is it? How are the vehicles? Are you sure where you're going? What does it mean to dream of a small Volkswagen or a large black limousine? And what are the differences between them? What does each vehicle say about you? What is the cargo of a large transport truck if you can't drive it? Why do large trucks need to be used? Is it possible to drive your vehicle onto a ferry and be carried across the water? Are you going home?

Maybe you see an airplane and a train in the same dream. What are your thoughts on train--trains-of-thought? training? You are on the right track or a strict way of sticking to one track only? What does this compare to an airplane flying in open skies? How do you feel about planes? Fear or enjoyment? enjoyment? surrender? What is an airplane, and what does it mean to be a train?

SETTINGS

Where is the dream happening? The land you see is yours. It may look like a tropical rainforest or a desert. Or maybe a meadow full of flowers and then an icy mountain. Your interior landscapes are seen in both the sun's scorching heat and total darkness. These views are essential in understanding yourself.

What are your associations with mountains if you have a dream that you are in the mountains? Do you feel at a higher level within yourself? Are you in a place of clarity? Perspective? What are your obstacles if you view mountains as obstacles? Are you moving with the current or against it when you find yourself in a river? Perhaps you find yourself in a desert surrounded by sand dunes. Your eyes are lost and your efforts make mirages.

Sometimes, you might dream of sitting in a courtroom and being judged. Sometimes you may even dream about a church or a temple. Do you feel the need to look inward and contemplate your purpose in life? You might find yourself at crossroads, or at a point where you must make a decision on your next steps.

These are only a few possibilities. It is easy to see how setting a dream can help you find your "where are you" or guide you towards what you should be doing.

WORKING WITH A SYMBOL

Participate in the creation of the symbol. Write down all possible ideas, even if they don't seem valid. When the rational mind is exhausted by the endless stream of ideas, intuition can be triggered. If not immediately, it may take a dream to trigger your intuitive perception.

Ask yourself if you can imagine a table in your dream. You can include the idioms that you use: a table to sit at, somewhere to eat, a table for a discussion, and a table where we can all eat together.

Here are some suggestions and questions that I received as I guided someone through a dream about the symbol bear.

Did you have a friend or family member in your youth who was like a bear in your eyes?

It is important to ask "Who is the bear?" but the bear does not always belong to the same person. You may also feel compelled to act by your very strong emotions. Perhaps the dream is a reminder that you have to confront these compulsive, wild emotions?

For some, a bear is a symbol of strength. Could the bear be a symbol of your destiny or a force with immense power over you? Could it be karma or a symbol of your destiny?

Look at your fears if the bear causes you fear. Fold a piece paper in half and note down all your fears. On the other, write where the fears originated. You may find that some fears are just the misperceptions of uncultivated minds and uncultivated emotions. If you look at them, you might be able let them go.

Write down all of the bear stories you know, starting with "The Three Bears."

Although a bear is an extremely powerful and strong animal, children have teddy bears. Are you a teddy bear or a friend's teddy Bear?

How does a bear's life look? What about the male bear and female bears, as well as the cubs? Is it too early to push a young bear up a tree at two years of age? Was it a push to get you in a difficult situation? Too soon?

Spend some time contemplating the symbol. If you feel that a dream is very powerful, review the previous three, four, or five dreams to see if they can help you understand. Pay attention to the dreams that come next.

REFLECTION ON ONE SYMBOL

You might be surprised at the meaning of one dream symbol if you take the time to think about it for a week. Amazing new possibilities can be found when you are focused on the meaning of your dreams. This is an example of my dream about a spider.

The Spider and Her Web

Two trees were present, and a spider was creating a web between the branches. The sun was shining on the silk, as it was still early in the morning. A few tiny dewdrops shimmered like honey drips. The spider began pulling the thread in itself. It decided to move on to another place because it had not caught any food or other edibles. It pulled in the thread as I was fascinated. The spider pulled in all the thread and moved on to the next location. It laid out the web's circumference first, but the web is not always perfectly round.

I knew that this was what I saw when I woke up, before the web was even finished.

Process in real life too. The symbol was then a subject for reflection. What could it possibly signify? Do I spin webs? Is there someone else who spins a web? Is it the spider?

It was something I thought about for over a week. It was a wonderful lesson that the spider had taught me. It locates a spot and makes a web to catch the food it needs. It suspends itself in midair until the wind blows to it where it can stay. It is the same in spiritual life. It is the beginning of something. It is a thin thread. It can break in the breeze of life at any time. It can grab something from the spot where it has secured the thread, and it could dangle dangerously. My first meditation was the beginning of my journey to finding something. I went to India holding onto my faith. [10]

The foundation of the web is formed at the first four to five points where the spider joins it. It then walks along and spins the threads to capture flies or moths. It creates a spiritual net and finds inspiration and transcendent ideas in it. These ideas are ours once they are in our net. The spider eventually pulls the silk out of its web because it can't find enough food. It then finds another place and starts the process again. We turn to other practices when certain practices become repetitive in our search for spiritual insights that will sustain us.

Continuing reflections on the web and the spider helped me to understand the symbol. The dream occurred while I was teaching a class about the energy that the Cosmic Intelligence uses to create this cosmic play. I had some images of Divine Mother Kali who gives birth to one and then devours another, symbolizing the cycles in life. Although they understood the symbol intellectually it didn't touch them. I was looking for a metaphor to help me understand this complex philosophical view. The dream I had about the spider came to me.

You could also say "Look at God as a spider, because it is from there that the whole universe is made. The Cosmic energy is like the silk of a spider. The dewdrops represent our planet, galaxy, and other galaxies. All this energy will eventually be returned to the Cosmic Intelligence and spun out somewhere else.

Astronomers speak of black holes, believing that all things will eventually collapse. This will condense its energy and make it so dense that it cannot reflect light. What will happen to the black holes? It will expand and create new galaxies. New planets. New asteroids. Stars. The cosmic cycles go on.

My little dream spider had a big message.

DO NOT IDENTIFY WITH THE SYMBOL

When you are working with your dream symbols, I recommend that you don't identify with any of them, whether animate or inanimate. While some people believe that you should identify with all images in your dream, spiritually this can help you strengthen concepts you want to release. Do not attempt to be the tree if you have a dream about it. Trees cannot move because they are deeply rooted and can often be confused with other roots. You are strengthening a physical connection to the Earth by identifying with a tree. Instead, ask yourself "What does a Tree mean to Me?" Look at the meanings of the symbol until it becomes too fragile for you to see.

Although you can see the symbol's energy, you cannot identify with it. Because my level of consciousness differs from hers, I wouldn't identify with a dog in a dream. A dream object, such as a crystal bowl or a chandelier, can only communicate a message. I don't want to identify with anyone but my Higher Self, or inner Light.

It is very delicate to identify. It is a delicate thing. We often confuse it already. You will never find your divinity if you are unable to identify with other people and objects. Find out what you are most drawn to. You should not identify with the most dear and personal to you, your own body. Your true dignity is found in your Higher Self, your inner light, your Buddha nature or your soul. Think about what your soul is.

DREAM SYMBOL DICTIONARY

We can gain valuable guidance from dreams and also see the vast range of symbolism in our own dreams. Each dream's key symbols should be copied with the meanings that they have to you. Then, at the end each month, put the symbols alphabetically. This is possible if you have a computer. You will see results if you are willing to work hard. This process will reveal a lot about your mind's functioning.

As you learn more about the symbols, expand the meanings. It doesn't suffice to know what "tree" means two years ago, or even two months back. Even if you make every effort to change, the meaning of "tree" may not be the same as it was two years ago. You can find the evolution of symbols in your dream symbol dictionary by looking through it.

You may find clarity when you examine the meanings of symbols as you work with them. If you think of water, you might begin by writing down the associations. Later, you will think deeper. What is the water of life? What sustains you? Water--emotions - calm or rough? Water under the bridge--nonattachment. Water--fountain for youth--memories from old fairy tales Water of immortality? Water for illusions, for the mind--clear and murky? Water to quench my thirst - the thirst for life, spirit?

It is possible that you have moved beyond the original meanings of the symbol. You may be able to see the various levels and enter the intuitive mental space of dawn or dusk.

You will see how your unconscious uses your words to convey important messages as you build the dictionary of your unconscious. You will gain clear insight through your efforts to learn your language. This will allow you to be independent from the opinions, judgments, and criticisms of others. You can also use your dream symbol dictionary to show how you have evolved, which can greatly improve your self-image. It's like discovering treasure in your backyard.

chapter 5

INTERPRETING DREAMS

Once you've explored each symbol, it is time to take the time to look at the whole dream, taking in all of its elements. This is similar to standing on a rooftop looking out at the ocean. You have a wider vision than when you sit in the kitchen where you can only see the ocean. Even if you don't understand the whole message of a dream you can still work with it to find the inspiration to think. You'll gain insight that will improve your self-image, and help you get closer to your goal.

You may be able to see twice as much if you look at the same dream a year later. The Higher Self won't keep you waiting if you try to understand. It will show you the missing messages from another set of dreams, just like beads on string. It will show you where to go. The first step is to dream.

Acceptance of the unconscious is key. Both the positive and negative must be dealt with. Both the positive and negative can be considered one unit. You may find that something is only temporarily annoying you but not necessarily negative. We must learn to discriminate.

Although dreams are gentle, they can make us work. Your Higher Self will send you the dream in a specific way because it is important. The reason must be discovered. Dreams need to be worked out carefully. Do not hesitate to write down your first impressions, but avoid giving too many quick answers. Seek out the true message of your dream. You might miss out on the immediate help that is available if you don't pay attention to its significance. The help may be delivered in six months, one year or two years. However, the message could have been very helpful in the interim.

The dream doesn't wave a hand and say "You bad girl." This is what you did. "Look--terrible!" The Higher Being isn't judgmental. It warns, "Better to be cautious." You could easily injure your head if there is a chunk of rock sticking out." The dream then leaves it up to the dreamer for them to discover the meaning of that rock. You will find the meaning if you work with the dreamer and cooperate.

The Higher Self is the most generous. It will tell you exactly what you need to know, but it will not hurt you in any way. You become more courageous. You will become more open to seeing the messages in your dreams. Dreams can sometimes exaggerate to grab our attention. Just like children's stories are embellished to grab their attention and hold it, so too is the story of a child. It is easy to forget a short dream. It might be lost if it is too long. However, it will still intrigue us.

We can receive a simple message if we are courageous enough to let go of our ego. The unconscious will only allow us to accept what we are able and willing to handle. This is a very important point to remember. You can ask for your dreams' to be concise and direct. This is if you are able to make them real. If you truly want to understand the message of a dream, you can see it in a flash. Your Higher Self can tell you, "Now, there's no mistake, it's what it means," in your dream.

Let me give you an example of a dream I had.

The Five Children

When I entered a room, I saw a woman sitting at a round table having breakfast with five of her children. The youngest child was a baby that was sitting on the mother's lap, banging its spoon. After they had finished eating, she sent the four older kids off to school. As she held the baby in her arms, she said to me, "You will always remember your dream." This dream is very important. Don't forget it. It is your five senses. I will help you interpret it. You are neglecting the fifth sense, which is hearing. Four of them have been trained and are now going to school.

Listen to your inner voice. Listen to the inner voice with your third ear.

I received amazing instructions from the dream. It gave me the exact instructions I needed. Although I was working on developing my senses at the time, it never occurred to me that one could develop "a third hearing," which is a sense that hears the voices of the voice. This sense has the most exquisite perception.

A week later, I was practically pushed to develop workshops that have become the basis of teaching at the Ashram. The program had been advertised for nearly a year and had already been offered by several psychologists. They called the night before they were due to arrive to inform them that they were stuck in Mexico and couldn't make it. What could I do to help them? I couldn't give them a psychological workshop and I couldn't offer anything too Eastern. Who would? Could I translate the Eastern approach of symbolism into Western terms? This is how I started my first workshop for self-development to help people understand their personal symbolism. [11]

That was when I realized why I had dreamed. I would have to listen with my third ear during the workshop. That's what I did. I asked questions, got the information from the individual and continued to listen, asking questions.

Say thank you after a good dream. You will have clearer dreams if you can say "Thank you". Recognize your Higher Self. Your dreams should be your top priority. This will make it easier to understand. The more you cooperate, the more you will get. First, you must give. It's similar to being in an academic conservatory. The more challenging the studies, the less students. If you don't put in the effort required, how can it be possible to become a virtuoso. You shouldn't be handed the opportunity to achieve this achievement. You don't have to be born with talent.

Clear dreams can be achieved by praying. We are often so confused by the situation that we have to pray to receive the strength to face it. It is important to be both courageous and humble. We must be brave enough to face the messages, but humble enough to recognize that Grace is needed to help us deal with all of these problems. Grace will come when we recognize that Grace is needed. This is when our lives can truly change.

The unconscious works hard to convey the message. Every dream is an effort. Every dream has a meaning. Although some dreams seem to be merely a review of the day, they actually have a message to send. If you dream that you do the same thing as you did the day before, you may dismiss it. Your mind might be just being repetitive and mechanical. Look beyond the obvious. Imagine that you are required to design pamphlets or letters for your job. In your dream, you do this. You will be able to tell if the dream is showing you a different way to accomplish the task, or if it is faster or better quality.

In dreams, there is no meaningless or extraneous thing. Each part is important. You just need to pay more attention. You may dream of getting invoices and putting them on the computer. This is exactly what you did all day. Simply put, writing a bill. I would ask, "If you received many bills, did they get paid or were they just stored on your computer?" A dream could also be the catalyst that gets you thinking about all the debts you have. It is possible that you have not recognized the karmic debts that you must pay. [12] You may not have recognized the karmic debts you need to pay.

You might find that your intellect (or the computer) has led to too many debts. This might be something you should consider if you were guided by your heart. You might then have a flashback to the word "voice" or invoice: I need to listen to my inner voice.

Don't assume that dreams are just repetitions of daily activities or that they come from some lower part of your mind. In order to convey a message, the unconscious may use language you already know. If you want to connect with the God or guru within, be serious about your dream work. These words are lovely, but they don't have any practical application in everyday life. To determine if you truly desire to be a spiritual being, take the time to really examine yourself. It is not easy. You also need to evaluate yourself.

If you reject a dream the first time, the message it contains will not be repeated. Your unconscious is extremely creative and may present the message in different ways until you finally understand why you have six dreams in succession. You can be sure that all six of those dreams had the same message.

One student brought a series dreams to class that she couldn't understand. She appeared in court and was ordered to remove her clothes. She thought she couldn't stand naked in this place. In her second dream, a police officer told her to remove all her clothes. Next, she had a dream where she visited a friend and invited her to go swimming in her pool. However, she didn't have a bathing suit with, and was actually wearing a fur coat. She was called by her friend to join her in the pool. The water is stunning. Don't be afraid to take off your furcoat. You can also take off your clothes. It doesn't really matter.".

In her dream, she was in a motel with her friends surfing. They wanted her to go along, but she was naked. It's amazing!" She didn't. She returned to her dark motel room and went to sleep. She began to hear strange sounds and was afraid that someone might be trying to enter her room or peek through the window.

This woman was a therapist and worked as a counselor in her everyday life. She asked other people to share their fears and problems with her. However, her fear of judgment, criticism and exposure was overwhelming. She was shown in dreams how reluctant she was to be naked. If she did, she would have a better understanding of other people's problems and a greater freedom. The whole class was able to understand the message instantly when she read them out loud.

It is better to work on a number of dreams than one. It is risky to focus on one dream and then to evaluate your entire life from the image it has created. This would be unjust. It is unfair to say that you are only limited by what one dream shows. Even if your dream points out a terrible mistake, you are still more than that one dream. Everybody makes mistakes from time to time. We learn through trial and error. Always consider multiple dreams.

If you have a dream that recurs throughout your life, it is likely that it contains an extremely important message that you are not aware of or have understood. Take all the dreams that recur and examine them carefully. Before you go to bed, think about what the messages are.

Sometimes, we can understand all of a dream but only a small portion. This is what happened to me in this dream.

The House with a Huge Foundation

As I was walking along a highway, I noticed a cliff made of solid rock. It contained a large foundation that would support a house being built. Is this the foundation for this house? The house is anchored on rock and then cedar trunks of huge size, as tall as me. It's amazing! The foundation of this house is amazing. It was built on rock and has those huge cedar logs that don't rot. I want to find out who lives there. Perhaps I'll ask them if they would like me to see their houses.

I climbed up the hill to reach the door thinking, "This is a wonderful house." It was a great foundation, rock and cedar.

It didn't appear that there was anyone else than workmen. One of the men turned around and said, "The house is very strong. Would you like to see it? It will become your home. It's your home." "My home?"

Oh my goodness! That foundation!

I walked into a large, beautiful room. He said, "There are many more rooms." Continue on through. You can see that there is new paint on the doorframe. "It's still wet." However, while he was saying that, I noticed a slight streak of white paint on the coat.

He said "Oh, we can clean it up," and then dipped a towel into paint remover, and quickly wiped it off. But be careful.

I thanked him. I then went through the house. It was amazing--big rooms and big windows. It brought me immense joy.

It was an exhilarating feeling when I woke up. This is a great foundation! Perhaps I didn't have to worry about my mistakes as much as I thought, and maybe some of the criticisms I received weren't applicable. My spiritual home has a solid foundation. It was a great boost during a difficult time. It is sometimes the most rewarding job you can imagine if you love people and want to help them.

I couldn't grasp the meaning of the white paint. It is, at least, white. It doesn't have to be so bad. I'll just leave it as is.

Six months later, I had another dream:

The Affirming Song

One voice sang the lyrics of a popular song "I believe in God's goodness for all". Then, someone gave me a piece paper with a date.

When I woke up, I remembered the numbers. So I remembered the numbers and looked up my dream. It was the dream of the house with a great foundation and paint on my coat.

I suddenly understood, which is why it's so important to

Keep a journal or write down some details about your day and thoughts. The first dream occurred when we had just moved our ashram to the country. It was beautiful outside and I was thrilled to be able walk around our land with so many beautiful and new things to see. I didn't like being stuck at the typewriter, answering the same letters that were sent to me by people who only wanted to express their disapproval, their negativity, or their resentment. I was dealing the same problems over and again--people's selfishness. "My husband. . "My wife. . . " "My daughter is a. . . " "My son . . ." "My boss . . . " Everyone was to blame, except themselves. I felt somewhat resentful when I had to reply to one more letter written by a woman who refused to give up. I sat down at the typewriter, unable to think of anything. Then, I realized that I knew why I couldn't write. I am being too critical." To correct my attitude, I wrote a page of "I will not criticize."

This was the white paint. This was the error. Knowing the polarity in the mind, I should have realized I was strengthening my sense of criticism by writing negative forms. This was actually negligence. Instead of replacing criticism with more understanding and patience, I made a negative suggestion about myself. I had a second dream that gave me the positive alternative: "I believe the goodness of all."

It took me six months to get this help. We sometimes think that if we don't understand the message, we will get help in a week. This is not always true, as I discovered.

We must be very careful about what we see in our dreams.

Sometimes, I accidentally entered the wrong year when recording my dream. Instead of dismissing it, I looked up the year. What was the message for me? What was the message?

The dream does NOT say "Two and Two is Four and One is Five." If we are to receive the messages from our unconscious, we need to improve our intuition and interest in ourselves.

chapter 6

REVIEWING & CLASSIFYING DREAMS

Just as scientists check their calculations, so do we. We also need to review our dreams. Spend a few minutes each week to go through your week's dreams. This is a way to put self-importance, which can be misplaced in socializing. You will be able to offer something to others if you are able to become enough important for yourself.

Each year, take your entire book of dreams and make a point to spend a week reading it. You can also add your interpretations and insights on individual pages. You will become more precise and clearer with the increased distance between you and your understanding. This will allow you to discover your own growth process. You will be able to see the benefits of your own growth, even if someone tells you otherwise. Gradually, you'll begin to notice the changes in yourself. As a child, you will need larger shoes and bigger clothes as you grow. Only this is where you'll find bigger dreams. You will know that you have passed the grade if you keep your dream journal and add insights every now and again. You can now move up to the next level if you think of your life as a large schoolhouse.

Your dreams may have a new meaning. You can reevaluate all that has happened in your life by getting involved with self-discovery. You might discover that your faith and conviction have increased, as well as faith in yourself. This will help you to continue moving towards your goals. You will eventually realize that you are a different person. You can't reach this level without being ruthless and honest. It is important to get in touch with your gut.

Also, you must be humble enough to realize that your growth is slow--not by miles but by inches. To remind yourself of the lessons you've already learned, it is important to constantly review your dreams. You will be surprised at how many things you forget if you look back on your first dream five years or ten years ago. Reviewing helps you stay in touch with your knowledge and gives you another chance at putting it into practice.

Sometimes you may find a higher level of meaning in your dreams. You might also see that you were not able to understand and make misinterpretations or be blinded at times. You can then ask yourself "What is a Dream ?"-- especially if you are ready to see that everyday living is just another type of dream. List all the dreams that you have. You can then begin to group them into different categories. Because you want to learn more about your mind, the categories you choose must be yours. You will soon be able to identify the type of dream that you had by grouping similar dreams together and dream symbols. Once you are able to identify which dreams are anxiety dreams, which ones are prophetic, which ones are wishful thinking and which ones are instructive, you will be able to use your dreams as a tool for making decisions. This will allow you to increase your intuitive perception and awareness by systematically studying the unconscious process.

You have two options: either you can make copies of your dreams, or you can work on your classification system using a computer. You can quickly select key words and dates from your dreams by entering them onto a computer. You could choose to examine all your friends, family members, and acquaintances. You can then study each category. How many animals have you seen in your dreams if the category is animals? What animal were you most likely to dream about? What symbolic meaning does that animal have to you? What are its characteristics?

You can trace your personal growth by looking at the symbol in detail. You might find that many of the houses in your dreams were once quite fragile. Then they became stronger. Perhaps there was once an empty room; this could be a sign that you don't need to worry about that particular room. Perhaps a small, cramped house has been expanded by new additions. It is possible to see your entire life in a simplified way and make an assessment of your current situation.

It may be helpful to examine dreams that have similar symbols to try and condense the messages of multiple dreams into one. Although the message might have been repeated many times but you didn't understand it,.

You may only choose to use a handful of major categories in your dream classification, such as psychological dreams or instructive dreams. You can also create as many categories of dreams as you like. You could have categories like: Food, Health, Sex and Spiritual Guidance and Inspiration, Memories and Past Lives.

Dreams can be grouped together in color, vivid dreams, black and white, or both.

In your dreams, examine your senses. What senses were most active in your dreams? Are you able to hear people speaking in your dreams? Are you able to see and hear them simultaneously? How about touch, smell, and taste? These senses are you able to experience in your dreams? What senses are missing? You can group together dreams that have the same sense active. This will allow you to identify which sense is dominant and which ones need development. It is possible to see how your senses interact and compete.

Moses Maimonides, a twelveth-century Jewish philosopher, divided prophecies into twelve levels and provided examples of at most one dream or vision from each category in the Old Testament. You may find it satisfying to subcategorize your dreams in a similar fashion. This will give you a great understanding of your subconscious. This list could include: Precognitive Dreams and Telepathic Dreams; Clairvoyant Dreams; Warnings in Dreams; Premonitions about Your Own Death.

When you are working with your classification system, keep one set of dreams in chronological sequence. The order you keep your dreams is important, just as it is important for how your life progresses. When you're only 40 years old, you wouldn't celebrate your sixty-fifth. Your life is structured in a specific sequence. By following your dreams, you can see how your life flows and the way you are open to receiving. It is often beautiful to see how your Higher Self works hard and what happens when your Higher Self cooperates with you.

> The interpreter can go on forever, which is why there are so many dreams. We don't always get it right.

You will find that your subconscious has a very specific language when you discover what dreams are telling you. You will find it easier to interpret the language once you have learned it. Your Higher Self will also help you avoid making silly mistakes that could slow down your progress if you are committed to spiritual life.

The following chapters are: "Dreams Of Enjoyment, Suffering and Birth

Death," "Nightmares," Decision-making Dreams," Prophetic Dreams,"

I will be examining more options for categorizing dreams, including "Warning Dreams", "Dream Sharing", "Past Lives and Dreams", and "Dreams of Spiritual Guidance". To illustrate the principles and encourage you to think and investigate, I have included examples of my dreams as well as those from others. To increase your self-knowledge and awareness, it is important to classify your dreams according to what you have learned from them.

chapter 7

DREAMS OF ENJOYMENT, SUFFERING, BIRTH & DEATH

It is possible to gain insight into both our spiritual and emotional lives by looking at the emotional reactions we have in our dreams. From despair to joy, and seeing the opposites of birth and death.

We will always have emotions as long as we live in a human body. But we can't let our negative emotions take us away. Many tragic cases show that a feeling like revenge can last for generations, causing family disputes or religious conflict. The foundation work, or self-examination that I refer to as "the foundation" can help us achieve balance in our lives. It removes many of the obstacles that prevent us from reaching the Higher Self. It is important to recognize when emotions are overwhelming us and to take action.

You will gain new insight and a wider awareness as you grow. You will begin to recognize the subtler emotions of your heart and the sensitive emotions that caused you pain. While emotions can feel a great deal of pain, the heart will feel a sense of sadness. We will learn from the dreams we have what to do and how to look at things.

Sometimes dreams can be about reliving an unpleasant experience or pleasure, or the release of emotions we have not dealt. We are endowed with consciousness so we can look at our dreams to find out why we are crying or laughing.

It is possible to have dreams that make us suffer. Ask yourself:

"What is the pain?" Is it real pain? "Am I only being inconvenienced?" You may feel hurt and even cry if you are. Which kind of tears are you able to shed?

Self-pity, healing, grief, bitterness? Learn what's behind your tears.

Sometimes you might cry in your sleep, and then wake up crying. It is important to recognize the signs and symptoms of a nightmare in which you are sobbing. You are suffering. You may be suffering because you are not being heard. Because it is hard to overcome pride without being devotional, I felt that even the poorest Hindu servants were better off than the most educated pundits. This is what your dream could be telling you: If there is no reason to cry, no one died, no pain, no other fears, or premonitions, it could be your Higher Self, your soul, crying out.

This is something you need to know.

Your positive emotions of enjoyment will reflect in your dreams. It was a wonderful time. It was wonderful. You feel happy when you wake up. You may have dreamed that you were riding the wavecrest in your dream.

Sometimes, when my life was very hard, I would dream of Krishna as a young child or baby. I would feel a great sense of joy and delight in these dreams, like the one below.

Baby Krishna

It is dimly lit in the room I'm in. It is very dark in the corner, but I can see something on the floor.

Oh! It's a baby! There is no cushion! No blanket! It's a blanket?
The little one then crawls up to me and pulls himself onto my sari. He looks at me with loving eyes.

"Oh! You are Krishna!"
He disappears as soon as I recognize him.

It was a delight to see God as a baby and have him crawl to me. It was a great dream, one that brought joy and balance to my life.

You can also see birth and death through dreams. A baby can be born many times, which is often a sign that the inner self wants to manifest. Because it is small, this baby is not dangerous. Some people might panic if the dream represented a dramatic or significant experience. You might have thought, "I don't know anything beyond my mind" if you had a dream about the Buddha. It could be very dangerous. It could mean that I lose my individuality. What will happen to me? "I know only myself through my mind."

We may dream of babies and be told to protect them. You are aware of how vulnerable and tender the baby is and how much it depends on you. The same applies to a spiritually emerging life.

Many men dreamed of having children. These men were quite shocked. One of them gave birth in front a fireplace. I was curious why he did it in front of the fireplace. Is he allowing the baby to bask in the warmth of the fireplace, or does a part of him just want to get rid of the baby? He would have to decide for himself. But the implications were clear. Either he would accept and embrace what had just come into his life with loving warmth or he'd reject it. If his feelings were negative, he could at least acknowledge his hostility to spiritual life and admit that it was over. On the other hand if he responded enthusiastically--"It's great! If he replied enthusiastically, "It's great! I'm not a woman but I can give birth, so the fire will keep this baby warm!", it would be a sign that he is open to accepting the birth of a new consciousness.

What about death? Do not mistakenly believe that tomorrow will come. I have been in many dreams, and I'm still here. Someone else must die and someone has to be willing for it to die. Would you rather have that personality trait die? However, that doesn't mean you have to die. Don't wake up old ghosts. The past is history.

What if you had a dream that you killed someone? It is possible to feel upset and think, "I have done all these practice but here in this dream I have killed someone!" This dream could be positive. If the personality aspect you killed created many obstacles in your life, then it was necessary to kill it. If you identify strongly with the personality aspect of the deceased, you might worry about it and wonder "Does my dream mean that I will die?" This is a sign that you are attached to that aspect.

What is the motivation when you kill someone in a dream? What do your grandfather and uncle symbolize? Do they serve as a substitute for another person? Are you really ready to murder your spouse, lover, boss? These dreams can occur if you misuse language or say things like "I could kill that guy".

Look at the person you're killing. Consider him

arrogant? If he is, killing him would be a way to destroy your arrogance which must be destroyed. If you feel a strong need to retaliate, you should ask yourself: "What right do you have to attack other people?" Perhaps I need to confront my own arrogance first before I can attack someone else.

One of my most fervent Christian friends told me about seeing Jesus in a Catholic Church and realizing that I was contributing to his crucifixion?

How do you tell if a dream of your mother's death is symbolic or prophetic? You may dream your mother is dying if you work on yourself. Your old image of your mother has disappeared. You would likely act differently if the dream was premonition and not symbolic. You might feel anxious and may phone or write your mother to calm you down. Sometimes the dream's tone is a good indicator. Sometimes, it's very obvious that an image of an old person can be changed.

Sometimes a dream that is prophetic may not have a very distinct feeling tone. A few years back, I had a dream where I was showing people photographs. I saw several women in one photo, but one stood out more than others. But none of their faces were meaningful to me. One person asked "Oh, is that your mother's picture?"

I replied, "No, she isn't in the photo."

When I woke up, I realized that my mother had passed away. It was not a strong feeling that I felt in my dream: "It's over !"-- but simply, "She isn't in the picture." My mother was unhappy at the time I was born. She had not wanted children and had not been in touch with me since I received my initiation into the sanyas. [14] I kept her in my prayers, in the Light, and I felt that she would eventually move towards the Light.

Our current emotional, mental, and spiritual state can be reflected in dreams. This information allows us to take steps to achieve the promised results and overcome obstacles in our lives.

chapter 8

NIGHTMARES

Most nightmares are a sign of unresolved issues. People who have many nightmares tend to be the most resistant to changing their lives. They resist logic beyond all reason. They are stubborn beyond logic. The nightmares may disappear if the person starts to meditate, chant, or pray.

If you are having threatening dreams over multiple nights, it is likely that your thinking is flawed. You might have too much anger, too much resistance to positive influences, or a refusal of listening to dreams from the past. The threatening dream sends the message that "You either listen or you don't." Accept the challenge and accept it. Then, work with the challenge to meet your goals.

You may experience dreams where monsters or other forces chase you if you blame others and don't take responsibility for your actions. It is always "Someone else made a mistake." . . "If he was more intelligent or accommodating,. . . "You never make mistakes." You don't have to trim your selfishness or greed. It's always someone else's fault. People constantly blame one another in the workplace. Husband and wife are always at fault for each other. Many blame their parents.

You will experience one disaster after another when you try to blame others and refuse to take responsibility for your actions. Your own mistakes are your fault. Your life will become a nightmare. Your life will become a nightmare if you decide to not blame anyone else for the next three-months. Instead, you'll ask yourself where you were inaccurate, on time or if your instructions were unclear. You will notice that your dreams will change.

I know of one person who refused to accept responsibility and was always blaming others. She told me she had a recurring dream where a little girl wandered alone in a vast desert without knowing where to go. Everything seemed barren. The woman's tendency towards blaming others had made her life very empty and barren. She was like a child who couldn't find her way home because she didn't have a home.

The unconscious influence of people you blame can cause images of attack in dreams as well as symbolsizing your tendency towards attacking.

Find out who is following you if you dream of being chased. You could be very critical of others or have a problem with your waking life. One of your personality traits or one of your personal characteristics could be causing you to be chased. This personality aspect must be addressed. It can be either conquered, or it must be nourished. This aspect can become a guide for you on your spiritual path if it needs to be fed.

Sometimes nightmares are warnings about selfishness. This monster might be running after you and trying to eat your life. The dream's dramatic effect conveys the message, "It's your turn!" Get moving. Your life will be more fulfilling. Give back to your life!

One of my students had dreams about men abusing or attacking her. After working with her dreams for many years and facing her fears courageously, she finally had the following dream.

The Man Crouched in the Sewer Pipe

As I was walking by a large sewer pipe, it was on the ground. It was dark and there was someone crouching in it. I was he about to attack? My instinct was to flee. Then, I decided to look in and saw a horrendous, violent man. As I continued to look at him, he pulled a mask from his face. Underneath looked very friendly and pleasant.

Her dream was as follows: "Ofcourse I felt a sense of acceptance and great relief. The dream clearly stated that the dreamer was telling her that she could see the worst parts of herself and acknowledge them, and then find beneath them a friend or helper. These threatening characters I dreamed gradually turned into friendly, helpful aspects that I could call upon for assistance.

You can wake up if you have nightmares that seem threatening. You can tell yourself that it's a dream. Instead of fighting the darkness, invite the Light into you mind. Look up to the Light, because darkness won't follow you into Light. However, if your goal is to defeat evil, it will pull you down. When you wake up, you will realize that you have two choices: to go into darkness or the Light.

While some people don't know they're dreaming, others can awaken from a nightmare. Others can also wake up from a dream, while others who are aware that they are dreaming can alter the course of the dream. Different temperaments can do different things.

The following dream was experienced by one woman:

Big Waves

I was looking forward to going to the beach and taking a dip in the pool at a resort. The water was calm but then suddenly there were huge waves. I hid in my corner, afraid that I would be dragged out to the sea. The tiny lake was now a turbulent ocean.

The woman confessed that she felt crushed by the "big waves", the sudden changes and emotional dramas, as she worked with the dream. I assisted her in exploring options. I helped her to explore other options. How did her emotions create such tumultuous circumstances? She made a conscious choice to explore her options. She didn't have to be paralysed by fear.

A child who wakes up frequently with nightmares is a sign of great insecurity. Parents need to find out what their child is afraid of. You can gain valuable insight into your child's fears by listening to them.

If you are having nightmares a lot, it is time to explore your fears. You can free yourself from the psychological tension that causes nightmares by working consciously to overcome them. Clearing the space will allow for another kind of dream, a subtler message from your unconscious. Nightmares can be likened to an alarm. Pay attention to the alarm. You must take action to improve your life.

chapter 9

DECISION–MAKING DREAMS

It is important to be able to think clearly and not rely on your dreams when making important decisions. Sometimes dreams don't tell you what your decision should look like. Instead, it is important to consider your options and make a conscious decision. After you have made your decision, your dreams can be used as a guide. You don't have to act only on one dream. Try other dreams to see if you get the same message. This will ensure that your thoughts aren't influenced by wishful thinking or the creative juices of your mind.

Before you make any decisions, assess your emotional satisfaction. You will make sacrifices if your emotional satisfaction is sufficient. However, you should be able to anticipate potential problems. Consider the potential problems and limitations that your decision could cause. Next, decide whether you want to say yes or not. Let your dreams guide you.

For example, if you're trying to decide whether to accept a position as a university professor or if to stop teaching and become an artist instead, wait for your dreams to confirm or disprove the decision. You can say to yourself, "My unconscious already knows so please show me." Accept the dream as it is.

You can, however, oppose any decision made in your dreams for your own security. You can review the consequences of your decision and how you feel about them so that, if you make the decision to become an artist with no regular income, it is not too late to say, "Maybe I misunderstood the message from the dream." Perhaps I misunderstood what the dream meant."

Although dreams can assist you in making a decision, the unconscious will only be able to give it to you if you're open to it. You are telling your Higher Self that you won't accept any alternative to your decision if you don't open up to the possibilities presented by your dreams. The unconscious will not send you the message. Only the Higher Self will know that you will accept the dreams. You will not accept the other viewpoint if your fight or if you refuse to listen.

Let's say you ask "Should you stay at Yasodhara Ashram for just a few days?" You think "No." But then you think "No, this will cause too many problems." You might not see your boyfriend, or you might be angry at your boss, or your wife. But something inside of you says, "Maybe I should remain." It might help me to get rid of old habits." A dream will only help you if your desire is greater than your anxiety about the future or your family. The Higher Self won't respond if you don't want to hear it.

This is a toy idea.

Or, you could make the exact opposite decision. It is possible to think "I don't want to return home to that horrible atmosphere." I believe I will stay at the Ashram, where it is beautiful, the people are kind, and I don't have to do any cooking or dishes. It would be great if someone could tell me whether it was the right thing to do. It would be wonderful if the answer could come in a dream. The truth is that you will not get the dream you desire. If you are too afraid or ambitious, or have made the decision based solely on your own will or desire to escape, the Higher Being knows that you won't listen. Why say it? It is possible that you will receive the message in another time, perhaps a year later after you have lost the intensity of fear or ambition.

A dream that conveys fear should not be taken as long as it is frightening. You might find the answer if you wait and continue to investigate. The dream of an engineer, [15] showed that he was in a state of confusion when he tried to plan his actions. This would result in nonsensical outcomes. He could be led to postpone his decision until his confusion is resolved.

Your dreams may be so confusing or complex that it is difficult to understand, you might not want the answer. You can also create a dream through wishful thinking. However, you need to be able to distinguish between the different types of dreams.

People should always ask me, "What is the Divine plan?" You can open the doors if that is what you want. If you really want to do something wrong, it is possible to misinterpret the message. Pay attention to your daily reflections. Don't allow self-will to interfere with your daily reflections. You must decide for yourself whether you are ready to follow the instructions given by your Divine Being if you want a clear answer. The Divine can be told, "I will go where you want me and do the work that you ask." But, you cannot say that unless you are willing to do the work.

You will feel more confident when you make a decision based on multiple dreams and what you see in your thinking and reflections. You should only take action based solely on one dream if you're certain that you're acting from an inner level of spontaneity. You need to be able to distinguish between compulsively acting from an emotional level and spontaneously acting from an intuitive insight. Many people confuse the two, fearing they will lose their spontaneity. Your dreams can tell you if you've acted spontaneously, or if you've been forced to by your emotions and given too much power to your emotions.

My dreams have allowed me to make important decisions in areas where I didn't have any prior knowledge, like building construction or finances. Without their guidance, I wouldn't have been able to recognize the options available. My dreams have shown me when to enter a new phase of my work, such as when to start writing.

The following dream, "The Queens Dream", is an example of how God works with us and sometimes for us.

The Queens Dream

Six and a quarter years ago, I had been faithfully recording my dreams and working with them for six and a 1/2 years. But one night, I decided I wanted to go to bed. I was tired and tiring from the Ashram activities. I also thought that my dreams had given me enough material to last my entire life.

When I woke up one night, I realized that I was dreaming and I decided to say, "No, no." It's not something I want to put down. I want to go to bed. I feel tired. . . Very, very tired."

My dream voice said, "Okay, but write these two things down: Queen of the Bees, Queen of England." I fell asleep and found my pencil, and began to write the words.

They were so hard to read the next day, since I had written them in the morning.

I was dark and not in a cooperative state of mind. Finally, I deciphered my writing. It was the Queen of the Bees as well as the Queen of England.

"What can I do with these fragments?" I thought. Ridiculous. Is Elizabeth the Queen of England? I spent a year living in England, and saw Elizabeth's coronation. I have never seen a more sad queen. The mantle on her shoulders seemed to have made her feel heavier. What does this signify? Do I feel weighed down? Yes, I do sometimes feel weighed down, but it is not something I can't see. What does all this have to do the Queen of Bees? I don't know anything about bees. They are not my thing." I put the dream in a drawer and forgot about it.

Several months passed. One night, I found out that dinner was not ready when I arrived at the Ashram dining room. It was obvious that something had happened and I was eager to help in the kitchen. Although there were many people in the room, I didn't want to leave them waiting. However, as I entered the dining area, one of my guests insisted on engaging me with a conversation I was not interested in. He was tall and reached the top of the bookshelves to find a small pocketbook. Swami Radha said, "Oh, Swami Radha! What a beautiful book!" I would love to read it to you." I thought, "It's much more important to get in the kitchen and lend an hand." But then I was caught.

It's called The Life of the Bee by Maeterlinck. [16] This is what it sounds like. It was most fascinating." He stood up in the middle and read the entire chapter about the life of Queen of Bees. I was stunned. My dream was of The Queen of Bees. . . . This book was not available to me. It was one the books that had belonged to the previous owners, who didn't bother to take them up. But I couldn't understand how the Queen of Bees could apply to me. I was also distracted by the thought of making dinner, so I barely listened. I had a few thoughts that stayed with me but never got around to reading the book for myself.

You can now see the immense efforts that the Higher Self will make in order to convey an important message to us. One year later, I was invited to Oregon by an artist who lived in the country beyond Portland. This was the only time I was there. I was invited to dinner at her lovely home by her friend, who had asked me to come along on her way to San Francisco.

She placed a small envelope on my plate, and asked me to open it.

It was before she had even served the food. It was likely a question she wanted to ask or a thank you note. What did I find when I opened the letter?

"Dear Swami Radha, I just finished reading Maeterlinck's Life of the Bees and this passage really struck me. I felt the need to share it with you.

"I'm certain you will understand
why," Yes, I did!

What was it saying? The Queen of the Bees' life is very unusual. She is not comparable to worldly queens. She works because she has to, even though it is not an honorable or rewarding job. She seals up all the eggs of the bees and provides nutrition to them. She raises new princesses and they leave the hive at the right time. [17]

What is my substance? Only the spiritual message. I don't have any other resources to feed anyone. That dream must have something.

A very kind lady from England visited the Ashram at the end of that same summer. She said, "I bring greetings from your friends here in England." They were so positive about you, I wanted to bring something special. But I wasn't sure what you would like. You seem to have a very different life than the rest of us." She continued, "The only thing that I could think of was this: the first Jubilee magazine by the Queen of England."

It was overwhelming. This woman was the first time I'd ever seen her and I have never seen her again. I don't even know her name. On her way to Vancouver, she was here to distribute a magazine about Queen Elizabeth. . . Because I wasn't paying attention to the dream fragment: The Queen of the Bees, and the Queen Of England. It was amazing to see the Divine make such a huge effort to get his message across, even delivering the poor woman into the remote mountains!

The first thing that struck me when I opened the magazine was the fact that the Queen of England was the only woman who can't speak back. Next, I read that she is the head and first woman in the country. However, the work of Parliament's Upper & Lower Houses is done. Although she knows every detail of state, the queen will only make the final decision in very important cases.

The Queens' dream proved to be very important to my life and resolved some of the questions I had been struggling with for many years. I was trying to figure out how to distribute the work and did some long-term planning about the structure of the Ashram. I was responsible for the administration of the Ashram up until this point. However, I felt that it was important to give more responsibility to the residents. I wanted them to have more control over the area where they lived. Individuals who decide to leave the Ashram would feel confident and assured in managing their lives. They wouldn't feel helpless or stranded because everything was laid out for them.

Mixed feelings and thoughts were what I was thinking. Although I wanted people to be able to take responsibility, my sense of duty made me wonder if I was trying to escape a job that wasn't inspiring. After I first approached some people, I asked them "What are your interests?" What are you interested in? One person asked, "Would you like to teach?"

It was a difficult question to answer. Did I really want to get out of work that was actually mine? Was it just a desire to give up the parts that I didn't like? Did I become so ill that I couldn't do my job anymore? Was it because I considered myself too important to continue this work? It was what? These thoughts kept coming up in my head, and I wasn't sure what to do.

I dreamt a beautiful answer. This is how it is: There are structures in nature and human society that provide the right place for everyone. The dream implied that capable people would come to do the work. I learned from the Queen of the Bees that you should train more than one person, just like the queen bee has many princesses who will eventually start a new hive. How do I bring in other people? The Queen of England's political model should guide me. Let the issues be dealt with in the Upper and the Lower Houses, then be voted upon and the decisions made. This is how the Ashram works today. The dream confirmed that I wasn't trying to escape by taking on more responsibility.

My Guru wanted America to be dotted with small yoga centers. I visited them all, but it was more than enough for me just to manage one ashram. The centers began to emerge twenty-five years later, after my return from India. In this way, my dream of the Queen of Bees training the princesses to manage the new hives came true.

Can you imagine the effort it took to get the message across? Who does it? Who has the patience to do that? Who pulls the strings to make it all work? What made this man choose to read a book on the top shelf? The book was there because it was necessary. The woman from Oregon would have written the same passage and given it to me. The Queen's information was not given to me by the woman from England. It was a job that I had created for my Higher self to complete the message I refused to see, saying

"I'm too tired." I want to go to sleep. . . Two queens: Queen Of The Bees, Queen Of England. Ridiculous." You can see how absurd it was. It was the solution to the question of the most fundamental importance that I had been pondering for many years.

This was a dream that wasn't willingly accepted. Because I had been giving my best effort and sincerity for many years, it was a difficult dream to accept. But, when an important message arrived, my Higher Self insisted it be heard. My Guru was thousands of kilometers away and I couldn't make my students my confidantes. I learned to trust my inner guru, which was awakened by following up on my dreams. However, I did not try to control my dreams or predict their messages. Only the Most High could give me the message. Jesus said that "if you ask for bread, it will not be given you stones."4 [18] Your Higher Self will never let you down, even though you may not always accept. This is what I want you to think about and reflect on.

After accepting the fact that I wasn't running from my duties, I had one last dream about this decision.

Names on the Board

Walking along the familiar terrain near the Ashram, I noticed an unusually large tree instead of the ferry landing. A large poster with the words "Vote" was placed on the tree. There were also a few names of Ashram people listed. I read the names. My name was not on the poster, but there was a note at the bottom that the queen had chosen these people as the most qualified for the job.

I was able to recall three of these names when I woke up and I began to train these people.

This particular dream reminds me of the fact that you have a responsibility to listen and follow the guidance of the Higher Self. You will only want the Most High. Refuse to accept any other.

Only the Most High.

chapter 10

PROPHETIC DREAMS

Can we forecast the future? This question has been a hot topic in every century, and across many cultures. Some things can be predicted, like the ability to plant seeds that will produce a specific fruit at a certain time. Certain rhythms are used to predict the movements of the Earth, moon, and galaxies. These rhythms allow us to predict when day will follow night, which seasons will advance in a particular order, etc. Doctors can now predict, using modern technology, whether a child's unborn child will grow up healthy or sick.

However, can we assume that human events other than those already mentioned can be predicted? Is it possible to predict whether we will win the lottery, inherit wealth unexpectedly, be happy married, or win a contest for a high-ranking position? Can we foresee the future and predict what will happen in medical science? Is it possible for the human mind to see the play's outline in advance?

Of course, many predictions are not predictions at all. They are manipulations of those smart enough to understand how we behave when properly conditioned (e.g. in war, espionage, and politics). Because the last word will be what sticks in the minds of listeners or viewers, political opponents are in fierce competition for the final word in a debate.

What contribution does suggestion make to the fulfillment of a prediction. Some people are so sensitive to suggestions that they almost become hypnotic commands. Are there others who can see the future and are as keen to know what it will look like? How much do emotions play a role in this? This is another area that requires more research.

The best way to answer the question whether prediction is possible is to be our own laboratory. This allows us to observe our feelings, intuitions, and any unexpected, illogical thoughts that arise. There are many powers of the mind that remain unexplored. Some people may deny the possibility that prophecy is possible, while others believe in the power of stories. My observation is that satisfactory answers will only be found if we pursue our personal interests and are persistent in following through.

The doorway to this area is opened by dreams, which allow us to safely decipher the mind and its powers. We have greater access to intuition in dreams, which we only sometimes and poorly experience in our waking consciousness. Sometimes, dreams can be prophetic or "psychic", and we might discover this when we are working with them. The original Greek meaning for psyche was soul. We can view psychic dreams as a way of interacting more with the soul forces. To recognize these dreams we need to improve our observation of the unconscious and conduct a special study on the workings intuitive perception.

Keep a journal of your dreams. Note down when your dreams turn out to be prophetic. The mind will make things up over time if you don't keep a log. How do you feel when you wake up each morning? How do you feel when you wake up? Do you have an active or asleep intuition? You will eventually be able to tell when your dream is prophetic or symbolic.

Many people dream of a small, if not dramatic, event that will happen the next day. It could be seeing an object or meeting a person. You need to record the events and keep track of when they accumulate. Sometimes, the small events can lead to something much more serious. If you are extremely afraid, the small events can help you to accept this precognitive side of your mind. If you have a dream about someone in the morning, and they come to visit you later in your day, it is not threatening. You will be more open to possibilities if you have had a few nonthreatening experiences. The Divine is a gentle teacher.

Abraham Lincoln dreamed of his own death in a precognitive dream. [19] Lincoln dreamed he heard the grieving sound of many people. When he entered the East Room, he saw a display casket with hundreds of mourners and candles around it. Lincoln was assassinated several days later when he inquired who was dead.

Many people who are assassinated have some kind of premonition in their dreams. What is it? What is premonition? Understanding the interplay between forces is essential. If you plan something evil against me, I might feel fear rise and look around to find the source of my fear. Then, I will have the dream. Although I might not see the assassination, I could experience it in a dream.

Many people lived in the small village near the ashram and had nightmares that cars would plunge into the river as the old wooden bridge collapsed. A few people wrote to the newspaper asking about the condition and frequency of inspections on the bridge. The bridge had been checked for three months prior to the request. However, it was discovered that something had gone wrong.

A man's wife drove over the bridge every morning to work. He said to her, "I feel very uneasy." He didn't want him to go to work today. But, because she couldn't explain why, he ignored her feelings and went to work as usual. The car in front suddenly vanished as he approached the bridge. He braked hard, got out of the car and checked. The bridge was gone and the car in front had fallen into the river.

Scientistically speaking, there is no way to answer the question "What part of my mind tells me what I need to know?" Metaphysically, it is possible to say that there is a soul who knows everything. If people are open to it, they will feel the effects. They can't help but feel it.

When people are deeply connected and care about each other, communication can occur on a different level. This type of communication is only possible for some people, but it will be in dreams. The conscious mind shuts down the dreaming in the daytime. Because they believe in the power and ability of the intellect, they refuse to accept intuition. The intellect tells them, "No, it's not possible." There is no evidence. The message is rejected because there is no evidence.

We may be more attentive if the message is delivered in a dream. You may notice a different atmosphere in the dream, which is then remembered. Then you awake with this strange feeling and wonder, "Now, why would I dream that?" Before the intellect closes the door and dismisses the experience. Prejudgment can be delayed, at the very least. If these experiences are repeated and prove to be true, then the intellect might feel defeated. If you allow the intellect to win, however, you may lose your most trusted inner guide. This must be acknowledged.

It seems that men are often unable to see the truth of their intuition. Many war veterans told me amazing stories about their experiences. They would later deny the same stories four or five years later because their intellect couldn't understand them. One soldier captured in Russia was held prisoner, but he managed to escape. He was in a Russian town that he had never visited before. As he walked along a street, he came across a house that he knew was safe. It seemed familiar to him. He knew that there were 26 doors inside the house, and he knew exactly where they were. He was allowed to enter the house and found refuge from the occupants. He asked about the doors and was told that there were 26 doors in the house, but that two of them had been removed. This man later denied the entire incident. You can become a monster because of your pride.

We must investigate the time element in our dreams. Sometimes the reality of a dream will not be realized until many years later. The following dream occurred ten years ago, just before the Second World War. Because I didn't know dreams could be so important at the time, I didn't pay much attention to them. But this dream always came back to me.

Shrinking Bread and Worn-out Shoes

A typical German bread basket was what I used. It had a handle and was big enough to hold the heavy, heavy rye bread. Although the basket was the same size, the bread began to shrink until it became a small bun. It looked quite funny in the large basket. As I was walking, I noticed my feet. My elegant, beautiful shoes became so worn out that they were visible from my toes.

This was exactly what happened ten year later. Because we were so starving, only a small portion of bread was actually made from grain. The rest was made of sawdust. Shoes were not readily available. Every scrap of leather was taken to the army.

As I discovered from personal experience, dreams can provide instructions and solutions for problems that are not yet occurring. The war was escalating terribly and air raids became more frequent and intense. We were being bombarded with phosphorous bombs. The phosphorous would burn and spread when it touched skin. The following dream came true for me one night.

Bandaging the Wounded

A short, thin policeman pulled a man towards me. He reached out and pulled out a few bandages and a jar. He then showed me how to treat the man's hand, which was all covered in phosphorous and still burning. I was shown how anchor the arm and how to apply the ointment with minimal rubbing and touch so that the cooling effects of the ointment are best. Also, how to secure each finger.

A few hours later, there was another air raid. My friend asked me to stay with them because she was extremely scared. I decided to stay over with her even though I had my own place. On my way back, I passed the park where I used to go to the bomb shelter. All around were rubble and stones. The shelter had been completely destroyed by a bomb. I stared at the amazing circumstances that had saved my life from terrible injury or death, and was stunned.

A policeman suddenly pushed a small, muscular man towards me. He reached for a jar filled with ointment and pushed it into my hand. Help!" And I did. To bring back the memory of my dream, I stared at the ground and applied the ointment to the man's hands. I did not rub the area. I wrapped each finger with the bandage, as I was instructed.

These dreams gave me specific instructions that really helped me think. What is reality? What is reality? What is a dream? There are thousands of similar cases in wars. How does the mind function under extreme pressure? We seem to depend on the irrational side of things when we are under such pressure. This is what often prepares us for the next challenge. The following dream was an example of a similar situation.

The Burning House

Because I was the smallest person in the group, and also the lightest, I was asked to help. Someone tied leather belts around me and lowered me into the house. I then poured water on the fire and placed the furniture and carpets into the sink.

This incident occurred exactly as it did in the dream. Because I was the smallest person at the shelter, someone suggested that I should be the one who was lifted up with belts and ropes. It was something I had seen in a dream so I didn't have to be afraid. It worked in my dream so I was certain it would work here.

You will begin to notice that your inner guide, inner guru, inner teacher or inner light will respond more often as you work with dreams. You will then be able to believe in its presence. You will be able to tell when a dream has prophetic meaning by observing your dreams and classifying them, and then following up on the events in your life.

chapter 11

WARNING DREAMS

Through dreams, the unconscious mind can provide us with exactly what we need: warnings about the future, warnings about what is good for our emotional, spiritual and physical well-being, and warnings to help others. It is our responsibility as individuals to listen to this information and to consciously apply it to our lives.

A dream about going over a mountain or being near a mountain could indicate that you're acting in a way that will bring down a situation. This is what you want. This dream would be telling you to not go into business if you had it.

It would be like jumping off a cliff if you did not do the intended action. It's a warning: "Look!" You don't know where you are!

You might also be thinking about the burdens you carry in your everyday life. I have a wife and five children, which is more than I expected. To avoid being accused of being unethical, I'm going out and I'll leave behind some money. Then you will see yourself falling off the cliff. This dream warns you that if you do this, you will symbolically endanger yourself.

Even if you think you know what the consequences of your actions are, it may not always be so. Your actions could lead to unexpected problems in your heart, cancer or a fractured skull. Destiny may not always act through the same channel. It is possible to reach the end of your desires but only if you are selfish and self-centered, will your actions lead to some results.

Your "conscience" is the ability to distinguish between things. If you don't apply awareness when it is possible, your conscience will intervene and warn you. You can silence your conscience or make it stronger whenever you want. This is what we see in politics and business every day. However, dreams can send a message from your conscience. It may prompt you to ask "How am I exploiting someone else?"

It is important to think about what you want to do. What will you do with the dream? What will you do to act on the warnings that you have received? This is what one woman had hoped for.

Five Heavy Suitcases

I was preparing for a solo trip when I saw myself at a train station. I was carrying five suitcases, and no one to help me.

DREAMER'S COMMENTARY

I felt strong when I woke up. But I didn't know how I would manage all the baggage. I thought maybe I wouldn't go.

The dream was eventually explained by the woman to be her suppressed desire for a divorce and her fear that she would not be able take care of her five children (symbolized as five heavy suitcases).

My work with her encouraged me to encourage her to see the possibility of separation as a simple matter. What would it take to manage her situation? I asked her, "What were you doing before getting married?" Are you able to revive your career? Are you looking to improve your skills to be able to provide for your five children?

She became very angry at the thought of taking any action. She blamed her husband and refused to take any action to change her situation. She wasn't adapting or giving up; she was resisting. She had a dream that gave her the warning: "Will you be able manage all five of these on your own?" The warning was not enough to convince the woman to act. The situation won't change if people don't want to help themselves or just complain about their lives.

My first trip to India was my first. I wasn't aware of my dreams when I returned. I didn't make an effort to recall them, and I didn't have a method of working with them. However, whenever I had a dream in my mind, I would write it down. This was one of those dreams.

Protect the Baby!

From my heart, a baby was born. It was so small that I could barely cover it with my hands. The baby was being pursued by dark forces that appeared as a dark cloud. I was aware of it and quickly changed into a large overcoat to hold the baby close. I was now ready for whatever the future brought.

I was actually challenged by a group psychologists. They tried to convince you that I chose spiritual life due to the traumas in my life. But I realized that this was completely false. In India, I underwent a spiritual birth[20] by accepting my spiritual self and all aspects of spiritual life. I accepted this new spiritual self in me and allowed it to emerge.

The dream had told me to protect it. The large coat was necessary to conceal the new life I had just created. Also, because I was a new swami, I had to be cautious about sharing spiritual experiences I hadn't fully digested, valuable experiences that could be questioned by logic and reason. My spiritual self provided me with the answers I needed.

I explained to the psychologists that I had had some unusual experiences as a child and teen that helped me prepare for what was going to happen in India. These experiences were prior to the traumas they used to explain the situation. They couldn't accept these experiences because they didn't fit their expectations. I replied, "I'm a canary, but you want to make me a sparrow like you." But I'm happy to be a Canary. It's you who can't tolerate someone different. It is a challenge to your security." They were a little startled but I didn't get too bothered for long.

My dream had foretold me that I would be confronted one day. I knew this so I had already thought about it. It's like you are planning to travel across new territory. You look at the map and you know exactly what route you will follow. Although it may not exactly what you want, the preparation helps to avoid some difficulties.

A different dream came up at another time. I dreamed that I heard a rat chewing at the floor in my dream. I thought that it was a rat in the building, but it wouldn't be heard because it isn't visible due to the fact that there are three to four inches of wood. But the rat continued to chew on the wood, clearly not giving up. Because that was what I believed was the message, I had to take a look at my daily life in order to find out if anyone was destroying the foundation of the spiritual work. It could have been that I accepted someone in good faith, when I shouldn't have. What does "undermining" actually mean? It was a violation of the ideals of an ashram. It is not a good idea to live in a spiritual community that does not agree with its ideals. Once I received the confirmation, it was easy to take action.

Also, you can have dreams that warn you about food and health: "Don't Eat This"

“That is poison.”

One of the young men in the Ashram was a true chocolate lover. I was concerned about his health but didn't want to be like his mother so I kept my mouth shut. When he was working in a small shop, the shopkeeper said that his chocolate was old and needed to be thrown away, the young man inquired if he could bring it home. He ate chocolate every meal for the next week. He had a dream. He went to a shop to purchase a chocolate bar. The usual price had been crossed out. Instead, a large red sticker was placed with a higher price. Was that a sign that chocolate bars would be more expensive? No. His unconscious should not be concerned about this. His health was becoming more costly because of the chocolate bars.

Dreams can be both direct and practical. I tried pizza when it first became popular. It was a lot of fun and I wanted to be able to participate in the excitement. It was delicious and I only ate it once. It was that night that I had a dream.

Not Good For You!

A nice, big pizza was on a board. One big hand came and pulled the pizza away.

"Not good for you!"

I was able to pay attention to the dream, and I stopped eating pizza. It also taught me that I needed to take care of my physical health. My Guru used to make me very critical of myself. He couldn't eat this or that and I wondered what the point of yogic practices if they created such limitations. What I didn't understand was that increased spiritual practice causes a greater sensitivity in the cells.

Could the message of my dreams, in addition to referring directly to my physical and mental well-being, have also been symbolic? It could have been. It could have been, for example, if I was a young woman with an Italian boyfriend. The dream might have warned that this "Italian stuff" wasn't the right thing!

Another member of the Ashram wished he could make delicious sandwiches with tomatoes, lettuce, and other fresh vegetables from his garden. He dreamed that he was throwing the food into an outhouse. I suggested to him that this could be a sign that his digestive system was not making use of the food that he was eating or that he was refusing spiritual nourishment. I asked him if this was a sign that he was letting his emotions and needs dictate his life.

Both interpretations were actually compatible, as understanding at a gross level can often lead to investigation at a higher level. His body did not properly digest the food, and it was gross. It was also true that his body did not absorb the teachings. Sometimes a dream that appears to be about health can have a different meaning.

Every time I ask my clients, "What do your body eat?" Tell me what you feed your mind.

A Midwest businessman who was very successful had been diagnosed with cancer. Although he was already in bed when I visited him, he still had a pile of horrible books on his nightstand. I told him, "You must understand that your days have come to an end." Do you really want to bring this junk with you?

What are you feeding your mind? What can you expect from a mind that doesn't eat healthy and nutritious food? Self-control and discrimination are the keys. They are essential for our existence. If you don't work hard enough, you can't become anything. While we understand the principle of achieving anything in life, many people refuse to believe it when it comes spirituality and moving beyond their limitations. Sometimes, a person's life can be wasted by their attitude of "I don't have to do that." You do need to do this if they want to make a difference in your life.

The following dream was my own interpretation.

Share, Share, Share!

I had created a well-balanced meal that was scientifically nutritious.

In my dream, suddenly a voice said: "Share, Share, Share!" Share as you go along.

You can avoid costly mistakes and other wrong actions by becoming aware of the warnings that your dreams may give you. This is how you can cooperate with your unconscious.

chapter 12

DREAM SHARING

Most people find it difficult to grasp the oneness all spiritual teachers speak of. This oneness can only be experienced through the interaction between minds.

I recall a conversation that I had with a woman about the interaction between minds. She was about to lose her husband for a younger woman. So she begged him to stay and gave him her heart. But it had no effect. I was shocked when she said that her mind couldn't influence hers. It doesn't work." In this instance, it was her motivation. She did not want to understand the interconnection between minds but she simply wanted her husband to return to her by her will. He was already under her power throughout their marriage so it was the force he wanted to escape.

If someone really attempts to understand the mind beyond its normal functioning and really attempts to find the truth, then something can happen. Two people can have a beautiful conversation when they are open to one another and not trying to control the other in any way. This communication can only be achieved between disciples and gurus, and only when the disciple has the ability and willingness to receive. Many of the lessons I received from Swami Sivananda, my Guru, were beyond words. Sometimes he would ask the swamis for a large pillow to be brought to me at satsang. He would say, "Sit here ,"--and cover your face to keep people from staring at you." I would then receive knowledge of intricate teachings that was more clear than any words could.

If a group of dreamers works together for a long period, it is possible that several people may dream the same dream or parts of the dream at the same moment. This is a sign of oneness or interplay between minds. Sometimes, in my dream work with students at ashram, I dreamed of the other half of their dreams, much to their surprise and sometimes shock. This phenomenon, where one person dreams a portion of another's dream, is what I call "dream sharing" (or "mutual dreaming"). Here's an example.

Once, there was a rabbi who lived at the ashram. He realized that he could perform rituals and present doctrines, and he was able to speak Hebrew and ancient Hebrew a few months before he was to be ordained as a rabbi. His academic training did not teach him how to comfort those who are dying or answer questions about faith. His spiritual journey was not strengthened by it. He shared his dilemma with another rabbi who knew me. This man suggested that he go to Swami Radha's ashram in The Mountains after completing his training.

The young man asked, "What can I do to be a rabbi in an ashram up the mountains?".

The rabbi replied, "Don't worry. She will not try to convert. You will find what it is you are looking for."

He was there. I gave him the yogic practices, and asked him to look for the equivalent words and ideas in his religious traditions. Chant the mantra using elohim rather than hari om. [21]

Jewish tradition says there is no image or representation of God. However, the text refers to "Him", "the Lord" and "He," all of which are implying images. It was difficult for the young rabbi in many ways to grasp Eastern symbolism. He was able to understand the mind and explore it. He worked with me to help him realize his dreams. He came back several times to say, "I don't have a vision" or "I didn't bring a picture of my dream." I didn't notice the difference in his words at first.

One day, I asked him if he had ever dreamed of the interconnection between minds or dreams that went beyond the psychological level.

He stated that even though there was a spiritual branch of Judaism he had never experienced that type of experience.

I woke up one night after going to bed tired. I was wondering why I couldn't sleep, and if I should take a hot bath to get my body relaxed. As I was contemplating it, I thought back to a dream voice saying "Bobbe Bobbe." However, the next day I didn't remember it.

A few days later, at six o'clock in the morning, I was back in the office to prepare the mailing by adhering the stamps and address labels to the newsletters. I went through all addresses and began sorting them by state and province. I was busy doing this when suddenly I heard someone say, "Bobbe! Bobbe!" I looked around but did not see anyone. I thought, "Well then, somebody will be in soon." It's not important to me." I was focusing on the stamps and sorting letters while putting elastic around the bundles. I was only slightly distracted by this undemanding mental activity at the moment.

The voice said, "Bobbe Bobbe," but it continued for a while longer. The dream came back to me suddenly. Although I wasn't asleep, this voice called again to me from my dream: "Bobbe Bobbe." The voice then said, "Go and wake Jerry." Tell him that I'm here. (Jerry was my rabbi. I believed that someone must be in the kitchen or the other area of the house. So, I said "Jerry's still sleeping in bed."

"Well, get him!"

This was very odd to me. I looked around. I looked around. It was just six o'clock in morning. Everyone had been busy digging ditches to dispose of the waste fields so they must have been sleeping like huge, heavy logs. Something else was happening, I thought. I sat down and thought, "Is it a dream?" Sometimes I hear something, but I don't see anything. Now, I hear but don't see anything. Is there a state of mind that produces voices? Is this the voice you were looking for? It came from where? I wanted to find out.

Everyone began to slowly walk into the house at eight o'clock for breakfast. Jerry was among them. I asked him immediately, "Jerry? Who is Bobbe?" He didn't answer, but I continued to explain why I wanted to find out. "First, the voice appeared in a dream. Then, this morning, somebody said, "Bobbe, Bobbe" and "Go and wake Jerry." Do you know what that means? This morning, I wasn't asleep. "I was here working with the Ashram newsletter."

Jerry stood there, as if he was glued to the ground. His face turned white like a ghost. He finally sat down, looked at me, and asked "Can you repeat that?"

The whole story was repeated.

He said that he had a dream that he didn't want me to bring to class. Actually, I had many dreams that I didn't want to talk about. I didn't want to know. But now, if it spills to you, then I guess I will need to look at them." He stated that he had dreamed about his grandmother, whom Jewish children refer to as "Bobbe." She told him that she had guided him here.

He asked her: "How do you do it?" When I was four years old, you were my best friend. I can still remember your stories and the time you sat on my lap telling me stories. You've been gone for a while.

She replied, "No, that's not a mistake. I'm not dead. I am very much alive. I am very alive. I am aware of exactly what you are doing, where you are, so I support you with my prayers.

Jerry now admitted that he didn't want "to think about what it implied", so he did not bring his dream to class. It challenged some of his underlying convictions.

Jerry and I interacted in a complex interaction that involved a variety of forces. My help was needed more than usual to get a point across or to understand certain concepts. He was able to reconcile his dreams with my experience and dream, which helped him to reconsider. He came to realize that there was no end to everything and that everything is constantly changing. Everything changes, sometimes very rapidly and sometimes very slowly --sometimes too slowly to even be observed in one life.

A different way of dream sharing was when I received a message from another woman through a dream. My Guru Swami Sivananda would soon be leaving this world. The dream could have been too disturbing for me, or maybe I would have interpreted it as a rejection. So this dream was relived by another person and brought to my attention. Swami Radha, the dreamer, said that she was certain it was her dream. Swami Sivananda has never been in person to my knowledge. I have only seen him through pictures. He said in a dream, "Tell Radha that I'm giving Radha the coat she gave me." It will be mine.

Three nights prior to this call, I woke up at 3 o'clock in morning to hear, "Sivananda Sivananda." It was very distressing and I didn't know what else I could do. She commented on my visit to a friend's home, "My goodness, don't you smile?" "I thought spiritual people were always happy," I thought. By the end the week, a phone call arrived. It brought with it a clear message that would soon be confirmed by my Guru's passing.

These experiences lead us to wonder, "What is the mind?" Where does one mind end, and another begin?

chapter 13

PAST LIVES & DREAMS

To explore past lives and the hidden recesses of your unconscious, you must first clarify your reasons. What is the importance of this knowledge? You may dream that you will be able to access the information if you believe it would help you understand a weakness or gain strength in your current life. However, influences from your past life can only be considered a possibility and only if they help you achieve what you want. It would be foolish not to use something that doesn't help. You can explore this area as far as you wish.

Imagine that you are a successful lawyer but were a monk, nun or monk in another life. Your monastic past might have had a karmic impact on your current success. You may be viewed as very fortunate because you have respect and financial success, along with a beautiful family. You may believe there is more to life than this, and wonder why you think so. No matter what your salary or career, if the soul is committed to the Most High, you will never be satisfied.

There will always be an element missing.

If you discover that something is missing, and then go looking for it, influences from the distant future may return. It doesn't matter if you don't know the answer or can't prove it. It is crucial to discover the purpose of your life. Is it possible to find the purpose of life? And if you discover that the purpose of your life is to attain Self-Realization--even if you cannot quite believe it and even if you cannot explain what the driving force behind it is--still you may have enough curiosity and perseverance to go on.

The conscious mind will go in circles until logic and reasoning are exhausted, and intuition takes over. In due time, the answer might appear. Sometimes, dreams can bring back forgotten fragments. You may see a bigger picture as you piece together each individual piece of the mosaic. You may find patches that are not quite complete but you might be able to see enough to recognize the picture, and gain a better understanding of yourself.

Your past might appear in a compressed version in your dream, and it may reveal important information for your future development. As long as the message is received, it doesn't matter if the dream is a complete recollection of a past life.

If you don't feel the need to understand and know the past, it is not worth trying to find them. The past will eventually be revealed, which can lead to the acknowledgment of your mistakes. Accept that your past may have not been as great. You may have been unfaithful or abandoned the spiritual path. Maybe you disregarded the pursuit of the life purpose. You may be shocked by the details of the dream, such as the setting and the century, to realize that you have to move fast, that time is precious, and that you must accomplish everything you can in this life.

Although no one is required to believe in reincarnation it seems plausible. The opposite view can be taken, which states that there is no purpose to life and that we are just like apples that eventually fall from the tree. The unconscious might suddenly speak through dreams if you ask the question, "What else?" You may dream that you are standing in front a mirror and combing your hair. Then you might see a completely different face looking back. As you look around and wonder "What is it?" another face appears. After a while, you will be able to watch the whole thing with amusement or anticipation, but you won't realize that you are actually seeing the same face. It's you. It is you.

If you believe a dream might be about a past life or a future life, you should first consider how it could apply to your current life. This is how I dealt with one of these dreams.

The Herb Healer

A voice said, "You were once an Indian, and called by the people, Herb Healer." I knew that I was a male body and that I belonged to the tribe that lived at bottom of Grand Canyon. I was also told by the voice that you had the knowledge to heal all diseases because there are herbs for all of them. The cover featured a bird on one side and a five-pointed Leaf on the other.

This was a dream from a past life. How could I find out? Before I got into this line of thought, however, I looked at how I could use the dream here and now. How can I apply what I know about herbs now? We used home remedies from earlier times to help us during the war. Many of the remedies I learned from my grandmother were very effective. Perhaps I could recover the remedies and the knowledge she passed to me about plants.

I walked around the grounds of the Ashram, looking for the various plants that I could recall and their purpose. Clover, Dandelion, and certain types of thistles were some of the things I found. I then gathered all the edible wild leaves I could find and presented the ashram a new kind of salad.

What could I do more? What else could I do? Photograph them and identify them. Do you know their botanical names? Once I have all this information, do I give it to others or make a book? I began by reading any relevant books and researching the topic to gather information.

The previous owner of the property visited us around this time, looking extremely miserable. The man had severe sinus problems and needed to have an operation within two weeks. Poor man was extremely fearful. I could do nothing to help him. He was eager to learn about herbal treatments and I asked him if he wanted to try them. I showed him how to make an ointment using the same method I used. His condition was so good that he didn't need the operation. Even though I didn't conclude that the dream was a reference to a past life, I could see how there were many benefits to learning more about herbs.

A few days later, some of my friends invited me to Phoenix in Arizona. I tried to ask them if they knew anything about Indians who lived at the bottom Grand Canyon. Friends who have known me for a while became suspicious of my desire to find out something for specific reasons.

She went to town, returned a few hours later, and brought back a local magazine. It featured a story about the Havasupai Indians living at the bottom Grand Canyon. I couldn't open the magazine when she handed it to me. Every part of me was alert, every hair stood on end. I thanked you politely and kept the magazine until I opened it. At first, I didn't want to know. What would it signify if it was true? The fact that my friend had found the magazine and instantly confirmed the possibility that my dream could have had a reality in the past is an example of what I call "substantiation."[22]

Finally, I finished the story. The story said that the tribe was still two hundred strong, and that the canyon formed a larger valley. There could be no more than 200 people.

This was a frustrating, confusing and irritating position for me to be in. I used to dream about my past lives and then quickly found a basis in real life. What about all my other dreams? What if all my dreams had a greater reality than I imagined? Do I need to revise my interpretations of all my dream? Study them again. So I did. I started at the beginning, and worked my way up. I was able to see the amazing resources my dreams had given and the many messages I had not heard on a different level. It was an amazing revelation.

It is possible to dream about past lives. However, dreams that refer to past lives should not be pursued because we live in the present. We must learn from this lifetime. While some dreams are only reminders, others can be used as a way to remind you that you have lived many lives. It is almost like a guarantee that you will get more. But you must continue to evolve, because every life has its own delays. Each delay can be quite painful as you experience the human experience over-and-over.

After visiting many ruins, I had this dream while I was in Mexico.

Jubal and Incal

A very old house looked almost like a ruin. It had walls that were torn down and was covered in stones. Although it was quite rough, one of the parts seemed complete. An old woman approached me as I stood near an entrance that was covered in cloth. I was standing near an entrance covered in cloth when she asked me, in sharp voices, "What do your want?"

I replied, "I'm looking for two people--Jubal & Incal."

I was a bit short-tempered by her words: "I have lived there all my life, but whoever they might be, I don't know them." She said it must have been a long while ago. They must have been dead for a very long time."

Curiosity isn't always a good thing. I didn't even attempt to find out how these names came about after the dream. Perhaps dreams are a sign that we have been in this or that cultural environment at some point. Maybe we feel drawn back to that place to trace our past. You have to remember that although I may have lived there at one time, and my body may still be buried there, it is not like a dress that I have worn. It is a dress I have worn before.

Sometimes dreams can be a sign of a resolution to past lives. You might see yourself in a relationship with another person and then see accounts showing zero balance. This could indicate that the karmic debts you owed to each other in the past are gone.

Perhaps you are open to accepting people from many cultures. I was in this dream.

Embracing All

I was welcoming different kinds of people to a circular ceremonial building. The clothing on each person came from various cultures. Some people were dressed in strange ways that I have never seen in any culture. We embraced and embraced each other.

These were my personality traits. If that was the case, I felt satisfied as it meant I had successfully integrated all my personality aspects. If the dream was actually about past lives, implying that I had lived in each culture at different times, I didn't regret it because I welcomed them all.

These dreams stimulate curiosity. We don't have the answers to such events, but we can allow our mind to think and consider all options. This allows us to be flexible and adaptable. You will be able to see the unconscious present details and information in a way you are comfortable with. The Higher Consciousness uses language you have created.

chapter 14

DREAMS OF SPIRITUAL GUIDANCE

If you are open to receiving their guidance, your dreams will guide and direct you. You can choose to be open to learning and using your intelligence correctly or you can feel desperate when you are in such pain or trouble that your Higher Self is the only way out. Either you learn from the Divine, or you are forced to do so. The law of karma is then yours. You decide. Are you willing to learn the hard road? You can't listen to anyone else if you don't want to. To feel more pain, you must become more desperate.

If you are able to listen to your unconscious, then the guidance of the subconscious through dreams can be very valuable. Your Higher Self can give you the direction for your spiritual path in a dream, or series of dreams. Different people will experience different things. Kundalini might be the best path for you if you have a dream about going through seven gates. You might dream that you are walking through a park when suddenly you see an image or Tara of Buddha or Tara. The features could have been from India, Thai, Tibetan, or Thai. Fritjof Capra envisioned the subatomic world as Lord Siva's dance. This was what he combined his knowledge of physics and Eastern philosophy. [24] If your dream is of the Divine Mother dancing the dances of creation and continuous manifestation, then this is the path of devotion towards the Divine feminine.

There is no single way that works for everyone. There is one way that you can learn about yourself and help you grow spiritually. This way is shown to us through dreams.

Your dreams will remind you that you're on the right track. When you feel lost or helpless, dreams may comfort you. It takes so long to grow? Dreams can help you see the truth of your own growth.

After my trip to India, I felt that I still had so much to learn. I was unsure if I would ever be able to make any progress. I wondered, "When will my consciousness blossom into a great being?" How do I attain Self-Realization It's unlikely. It is likely impossible.

The following dream came true during this time of struggle.

The Golden Flower of Consciousness

A tiny seed that looked almost like a speck was beginning to take root. It was almost as if I could see the roots from X-rays. They were white, spreading and forming a network. A tiny shoot grew and then slowly, steadily began to grow. A bud appeared, concealing what was inside. It then opened up into two coarse leaves. The shoot continued to grow upwards for what seemed like an eternity. Another bud was formed and the leaves were unfurled. Slowly, the shoot grew and grew until another pair emerged with even finer leaves.

The sprout continued to grow and each pair of leaves that emerged was finer than the previous. Finally, a new kind of bud started to grow. It had many small leaves. The rest of the plant slowly started to open, but the large bud was soon lit from the inside. The Golden Flower of Consciousness, an exquisite golden flower, was what I saw.

This experience inspired me to pay great attention to Kundalini Yoga's crown, the thousand-petaled lotus. Although not identical, the flower I saw or dreamed was very similar to the lotus. It was clear that it symbolized metamorphosis, and gave me a clear message.

If someone, even a yogi, suggested to me that I follow the Kundalini path, I would have said, "Yes, perhaps." How can I be sure it's right for me?"

I was stunned when my Higher Self demonstrated this to me. It was because I created and created the manifestations. It was all natural and came out of me. I couldn't doubt it. Even if it was doubted, I would have at least been able to test it. Then I would know.

You will find out when it is time to worship in your dreams. They will take your to a temple or a cathedral, and they will show you amazing images that may disappear in the sky, or even become huge.

Spiritual dreams are milestones along the Royal Highway.

Sometimes you may dream that you see a tiny metal Buddha in your dreams. The next day, you will check to see if it is there. It could have been put in my pocket by someone else and I didn't notice it sooner." In other words, messages from the Divine are sent to you in whatever way you can comprehend.

Is it possible to find your guru in a dream? Many stories have been told about people who did this in the Orient. To find your guru by dream, however, you need to be in a constant state of urgency and a deep sense of homesickness for your spiritual home. The meeting with the Guru cannot happen if you don't feel the urgency. Sometimes, you might have a vision in your dreams that helps you to take the next step in your spiritual growth. It is not always easy to determine if the dream image is of an actual person or if it is symbolic that you can accept as your Higher Self.

Your intensity is a sign that you are serious about reaching out to the Divine. If there have been previous relationships, it is possible for the guru to project his or her self onto the receptive mind. You can meet the guru in your heart if you are sincere and intense.

Even a dream can be initiated if the person seeking initiation has extraordinary levels of intensity and receptivity. If the person seeking initiation has difficulty "fitting in" to his or her body,[25] then the teacher will be able tell that it is not the right time and there cannot be initiation in either the dream or the waking state.

You should question the meaning of the image if you're already in a relationship to a guru. Is the image a projection of the Guru's presence in order to convey a message? Is it an image or symbol of your Higher Self Is it a symbol of your Higher Self? It is important to be clear about what you intend to interpret and not just interpret it according your own convenience.

If you dream that the teacher is watching you in a judgemental way, it's likely that you have made the guru into a kind of policeman/policewoman in your mind. Someone who can act as your conscience in a very negative way. Then you can justify yourself and say, "See!" Your Higher Self might be showing you that your Guru is trying to find fault in me. Your dream is a reflection of your thinking and can help you to decide if you are comfortable with this relationship.

I don't believe that the guru is always with the disciple, nor that the voice of wisdom comes from the guru. This is what is often taught in India. Swami Sivananda was easy to recognize by his unique style of speaking, his Indian English accent, and his tone. It was my English that I recognized the message as coming from my Higher Self. If you are able to listen in everyday life, you will also be able hear in dreams, and you will then be able distinguish the voice from the Guru in your dreams.

This Way!

I was greeted by a thundering voice: "Radha!" It's enough. "Come out!" I was in a large swimming pool, having fun with many people. It was not a sinful act. He said, "This is the way!".

This was typical of the voice and style of my Guru. Swami Sivananda didn't use many words and his sentences were short and simple. That was all. I understood the message and knew that it was from him. I wasn't supposed to finish the academic program that I had started. I wasn't supposed to be in that pool having fun. My Guru had other things for me to do, and I couldn't be distracted.

Similar to the above, your subconscious may reveal which mantra works best for you after you have cleared your emotional issues. The melody may be heard in your sleep, and you might discover the correct way to chant it.

If we are open to receiving help, there is a lot available if only we look for it. You will find the amazing guidance and instructions that dreams can provide if you are sincere in your pursuit of them.

chapter 15

LEVELS OF DREAMS

You will start to notice the various levels of dreams as you practice watching them, analysing them, and learning the language of the unconscious. Dreams can reflect many levels: the psychological, emotional, and physical. This includes fear, delight, fear, and even a sense of faith.

Your dreams will show you exactly where you are. It's like looking into a mirror.

It is important to first interpret dreams at the level of daily existence. Only then can you see if the dream holds a higher meaning. If so, it is worth making the effort to elevate your mind to that level. If your dreams are also applicable to a higher level of reality, it is possible to be certain that your growth is slow, steady, and smooth. This is better than developing in spurts and then moving backwards.

How can you tell when it is time for you to work with your dreams more than just psychological reflections? You can interpret a dream differently if you see it in another way. Because a dream can have multiple meanings, it is worth exploring. The level of daily living is one. Because the window was dirty, I couldn't see through it. Another level: Do I not see my potential? What filters are I using? What is my vision for the Divine?

What can I only faintly see?

You have many levels of meaning. They tell you that you have several stages of development. It is possible to elevate the symbol language that our unconscious uses to communicate with us, and learn how the inner self expresses itself.

A "super message" is a combination of the messages from many dreams. You will be able to see all your messages as milestones and can determine where you are moving forward and where you are not. It is possible to see if your dreams were merely suppressed concerns in daily life and what psychological barriers need to be removed to allow spiritual aspects to shine through.

You must realize, however, that no matter what level your dream may be, it is still coming from you. If you are not able to hear the voice of the "you", the part of your mind that is speaking through dreams may not be ready to understand. Talking about "levels," while it can be misleading, could lead to judgmental thinking. You might assume that this implies hierarchy. It is important to remember that there are many levels. We have the skeletal, muscular, and digestive systems. But we don't necessarily identify with one. All of them work together. They all work together to organize and manage our physical existence. The same goes for spiritual and psychological dreams. We cannot also separate the Divine from the Human.

What is the difference between human and divine? What is the ego and what does it mean? The ego is not vanity, pride, or self-importance. The ego is the powerful force that holds our bodies together and all of our cells together. Our personality aspects are also tied together by the ego. If you take your time and focus on one aspect of your personality, the entire personality structure will be a bit looser. You don't need to worry about other aspects if you focus on your biggest weaknesses. They will all disappear.

Each reality is unique to the ego. While the world we live in has its reality, it cannot override our spiritual reality. It is wrong to say that you cannot be spiritual because it does not fit in with my success. Your success is not yours alone. You would not be able to win without the help and support of the Divine. Recognizing this requires a lot of awareness.

Our ego is part of the essence and divinity of ourselves. Anyone who wishes to tap into the eternal essence can find it. It's only a matter if you have enough. Although a drop of water is not the entire ocean, it still has the same essence. It is important to understand the depth of the drop and the ocean. You will never see the drop again if you return it to the ocean. If you insist on your individuality and refuse to merge with the Divine, then the ultimate union will never happen. It is impossible.

The human being is a vessel for the Divine to express itself. As individuals we are part of God. God lives in us. The kingdom of God is inside. If we don't come from the original source of Cosmic love, there is no way to have Cosmic LOVE, even in a small amount.

Your essence is always there. Even though it may seem lost, it is always there. You are always one unit. Each aspect of you is both human and divine. This complete unit is part a larger whole. One drop of ocean is still part the ocean. It does not become anything else. The ocean waves are the same as the ocean. This idea was presented in an unusual, simple dream I had many years ago.

The Brown and the Blue Shoe

One of the young men in the Ashram brought home a box with only one shoe. He was uncomfortable when I suggested that he return to the store to get the missing shoe. I asked him if he would rather go with me. I carefully examined the shoe, and then I went. The clerk seemed a little embarrassed, but he set out to find the shoe. He told me it wasn't in the store so he suggested that I go to the manager. He gave me the directions.

Although the store was well-organized, the manager searched for the second shoe. It was slightly hidden on the top shelf. I thanked him for his help and returned to my home. We compared the shoes and found that they were identical, with one major difference. The shoe the young man had was brown while the one I brought home was blue. He stated that he couldn't wear shoes in two different colors. He asked me to go back and find shoes in the same color.

The manager didn't even try to find another shoe. With a smile, he said, "Go back, think about it, we walk with one foot along the brown path and one on the blue path." I was walking home when I noticed that my shoes were also different colors. One for the earth, the physical world, and one for the sky, the spiritual world.

The dream stressed the coexistence between the spiritual and the physical. Harmony is achieved when this coexistence is balanced. To achieve harmony, you must overcome your fear of criticism. Otherwise you won't be able to see yourself as Divine. If you don't accept the Divine within yourself, it is impossible to accept it in others. You can't accept the Divine within yourself if you don't accept it in others. This is the inner crucifixion. By denying the Divine, you crucify it. Instead, it is better to crucify your ego. Your dream will reach the level of direct contact to the Divine if you are able to do this.

You may discover that your dreams are made up of many layers. You may get psychological information about your actions or recommendations, but the dream may also provide instructions on a higher level, such as a spiritual level. If a dream contains a deeper message, we should not ignore it. We are who we are and must deal with all aspects.

Imagine that you dreamed of seeing a beautiful orchid in your dreams. What would be the best way to classify your dream? How would you decide which level it is? You might look at your dream from a psychological perspective. The flower might seem delicate, and the leaves may be stiffer than leather. Is this a sign of a combination of sensitivity and coarseness? You might interpret that to mean you have both of these qualities. You might ask yourself, "What are I sensitive to?" To my pride? To my vanity? To my vanity? To preserve that sensitivity."

Is it just that? Even though you might have a solid understanding of the basics, it is important to not limit yourself to this level and miss out on another message. There are many other avenues you can explore. You can explore more if you consider the coarse leaves to be part of my human nature. Can the flower also be a symbol for my pride? Is there something in me that is flowering? It takes seven years for an orchid flower to bloom. Maybe I should persevere in order to allow my spiritual unfolding.

It is possible that you know that the orchid lives on water and air. This orchid is considered to be the most developed flower. You might interpret this dream as "It would have been wonderful if I could live on such simplicity" - looking after my body, represented by the water, and being supported by a spiritual atmosphere, represented by the air. These are the only two elements and not many delicacies or desires.

The leaves remain firm and strong.

This one dream can be transformed into a masterpiece of research. It is possible to discover where orchids are grown. There are many kinds of orchids.

Which one was it? Is there a similar one? Was it the same color? What was the color of the orchid? Did it belong to one of the wild orchids that cannot be transplanted or are they protected? This could refer to more than just moving to a new country or city. It may also refer to how you think about the city of your being, your city of life. You create your three worlds, which are the past, present, and future in Indian terms. You have the power to create them. However, you also have the ability to withdraw that power and destroy your worlds. You can enter eternal life, or your inner Light, when the three worlds collapsing. This energy cannot be destroyed.

You might find that you are more spiritually mature if you understand the dream in as many ways as possible. This idea may entice. Although you may not believe it, the dream might convince you. You might be tempted to say that you are not good enough because of your human nature. It's only your pride and vanity trying to be someone special. But, if you are able to see the spiritual flowering stage of the dream in your waking state, then you should realize that if it weren't for you, you wouldn't even know about it. The Golden Gate Bridge would not be found if you weren't on your way from San Francisco to San Francisco.

You may find that you can eventually relate all of your dreams to various events in your life, and then put them all together. Sometimes, however, you might miss an aspect of your dream because you don't think you have the right idea about yourself. People who are extremely self-critical can miss what I call "a Divine Message" in a dream. It is possible to receive a beautiful message or a glimpse into your future. It's amazing to see the unconscious trying to convey the message. Accepting it is a great help. No matter what you think about yourself. Try to see all possibilities.

If you have had many dreams, and have worked hard to overcome your shortcomings and weaknesses, you might experience dreams that help you realize that your waking world is no different than a dream. You can make a change in your life. However, it won't be easy because your intellect and reasoning, which are the same processes that got you through this stage, won't let you go. Clear dreams are a way to get there, but not in a year.

Sometimes dreams can become more real than our daily lives. We can see that there is a reality in cooking, caring for our homes, and other aspects of daily life. If we can dream, like one great yogi[27], that Liberation is possible in a single lifetime, then such a dream naturally is very rare. It is a different level of experience and has much more value.

You may find that the dreamer knows more than the daydreamer as you begin to work with each level of a dream. While the daydreamer might still be interested in the world, the dreamer may have already decided that "What's the point?" The path to the Light may be already marked.

chapter 16

AN EXPANDED METHOD

"Where is God?" Why do you believe there is a God, and why? How can you be sure? Is God in your backyard? How can you be sure that God will hear your prayers when you pray? Is God able to listen? Is it possible for God to listen? Is it so important that God should listen to you? How does your prayer get there How can you find the guru? It is a matter time or a matter of faith? How long will it take to pray? How long does it take to find God? To find the Guru?

My Tibetan Guru taught me this kind of non-stop, rapid succession of questions. He would pick four words that were significant to him, such as God, Guru, Prayer, and Time, and then he would constantly throw them around in a flurry of questions. This method broke down many deep-rooted beliefs and freed me from ideas I had previously accepted without further investigation. Our mental prisons are made up of false beliefs, misunderstandings, cultural and social conditioning. This questioning reduces the prisoner ideas and concepts, which speeds up awareness.

Once you have mastered the chapter 2 method of dream interpretation, you can move on and learn an advanced technique that is based on rapid self-questioning. This will allow you to dig deeper into the meanings of different words and their combinations. This method will help you to get rid of false beliefs, strong opinions, and deeply ingrained ideas from your past.

When people use symbols from dreams to help them, I found that they often list many other words as their associations. This approach is designed to break the Western tendency to conceptualize without enough investigation. It requires that you treat each word in your list as a key phrase or word and then investigate it through rapid-fire questions in relation to all other associations.

This is a great way to go into depth and connect you to something inside of yourself and ultimately to the Divine. Because writing takes time and your thoughts will come quickly, you may tape your questions. This spontaneity can be a huge help. This process for your dreams isn't as dramatic as that of the Tibetan Guru. You are probably using your own words with your dreams. These are your familiar territory, and a great place to start this work.

This example will show you how the approach works. The dreamer had a vision that began with "I am living at an Old Farm commune." He then listed the associations as follows.

I am living—

A part of, alive, awake, accepted.

It is quite a large number of words. If the dreamer is looking to go deeper within himself, he could take each word of his associations and ask himself questions such as the ones below.

You should not only read the questions but also try the technique by asking the questions aloud. It might be helpful to ask someone else the questions or to record yourself answering the questioner. You can have a lot of fun brainstorming the answers.

Alive—

What does it really mean to say that I am alive?

Where am I alive?
What keeps me alive?
What keeps me alive?

How do I know if I feel truly alive?

What happens when I feel dead? How can I make my body and mind more alive?

What is it that keeps you alive and keeps me afloat?

Awake— *I am*
awake.
What time am I not awakened?

Should I be awake?
Do I have to be awake all the time?

How is my idea of being awake connected to my living or being alive, and how?

Can I live without being awake?

Does it mean I am alive if I am awake?

Accepted—
It is so important that everyone accepts it?
Who are the extraordinary people I would like to be accepted by?
How do I know if I am accepted by God?

What is the best time to accept?

What happens when I accept it only mentally? Will I be able to see the value of acceptance when I am truly alive?

If I'm awake and aware enough, can I distinguish between what I want and what doesn't?

How far can I go to get accepted?

What are my ingrained beliefs that prevent me from accepting other people?

A part of—

So, I live, but I also am a part--the world. A country, a city and a work place are all parts of me.

Does it give me the assurance that I am accepted and that I am truly alive when I know that I am part?

Can I be part, but not be awake?

What are the barriers to me knowing I am part of something?

What are you looking for? This view is so important?

Active—

What do I mean?
Does it mean that I am active if I live?

What activities are I doing that isn't the norm, such as eating, drinking, or working?

What's my activity as a member of something?

Do I want to be accepted because I am active?

Do I feel active because it keeps my awake, alert, and alive?

Find meaning—

I live, I find meaning.

What is the best way to find the meaning of this sentence?

Is this meaning just for me or does it also apply to others?

Does this meaning relate to the purpose and goal of life?

Are activities or being part of life meaningful? Or acceptance or awareness? Does that make me feel alive?

Working—

Living means that I also work.

What is the difference between being part of life and activity?

What kind of work do I mean?

Working for a living?
Working on a relationship?
Working on myself?
Does it make sense to work?

Are work and activity related or different?

Do I get to be a part or a sub-part of another organization when I work?

Does my work acceptance guarantee me acceptance?

Do I have to accept others who work?

Can I work and sleepwalk at the same moment?

If that is true, then why not? If it isn't, why not?

What are the advantages of working?

Where are the benefits of working?

Do I work for my personal success or do I seek meaning? To be accepted Exploring--

Do I need to explore in order to be alive?

What am I exploring?
What is it that tempts you to explore?

What can I expect to find or gain from my explorations?

What if I work to explore?

Or can I explore meaning?

Is it just another hobby?

Would you like to take part in an exploration?

Do I feel more accepted when exploring?

Do I feel awake when I go exploring?
Does that mean I feel alive?

Giving—

I live, I give.

What do you give? Emotionally, mentally and economically?

Why would I give anything?

Do you think I know that I am alive?

Or should I give to be accepted?

What do I need to give in order to be accepted?

What is the purpose of giving a portion of an activity?

What does it mean to give?

Are you giving your work to a single thought or a very specific thought?

Which do you prefer, to give of yourself or to give money?

I will give money if I don't have a attachment to money.

If I feel attached to money, I might not want to give it; instead, I will do something different.

What is the difference between giving and receiving? Is it possible to call either one giving?

Serving—

I live, I serve.

What do I serve?
My spouse, my husband, our children, my parents and my friends?
Do you serve and give the same?

Do I serve to explore avenues around me?

Do I have the right to share the results of my work?

Do I have the ability to give myself a higher purpose, to find meaning in my life?

Is serving a way to find meaning?

What is the service of activity?

Again, I am part of something when I serve?
Do I feel accepted if I serve?

Feeling—

I feel, I live.

There are many emotions I can feel: happy, angry, unconcerned. Blessed, loved. hated.

All these emotions will I also share with others.

How much do my emotions influence how I live?

What is the best place to find satisfaction in my feelings?

Acting—

Because I act, I live.

Is acting and feeling connected?

Is acting and serving connected?

Giving, exploring, and working are all ways I find meaning?
Does acting involve serving and giving? Or is it a form of exploration?

Are they different?

What is the difference?
As a member of a group, whether it's a family team, a work team, or a friend, you can act as a part of a team.

Is it possible to accept wrongdoing or rightdoing? How can I recognize the difference?

Open—

Because I am open, I live.

Are I open? To find out if my openness is true, I must look at my actions and interactions with others.

Is it possible to be open in acting and in feeling?

Do I have to be open to serving and giving?

How willing will I be to explore and work?

Do I find more meaning when I'm open than when I'm active?

Do I feel threatened or able to be open with a group?

How open can I be in my daily life?

What would be the opposite?

Secrecy? Loving--

Can I love and be open?

Do I feel ashamed of speaking out, or expressing my feelings openly?

Do I feel loved and generous?

What does it mean to love my explorations?

Is work possible while loving it?

Is love a way to find purpose?

Are my actions a result of loving?

Are I more loved if I love?

Is it helping me to be more conscious?

Are I truly alive when I love?

Connecting—

What does it really mean to be connected? What does it mean to be connected?

What are the benefits of being connected?

Are I more loving when I'm connected?

Am I more open?
Am I acting differently?
Let my feelings be known?

Does it serve to connect me?

How would I connect with giving?

Connecting and Exploring--Where would it take me?

To discover the past, the future, and the present?
Is my work connected to me?

Do I find meaning by connecting?

Does connecting count as active?

Can I be certain I'm accepted if I am connected?

Will I need to be connected in order to be accepted?

Do I need to be aware and awake to connect?

When I feel connected, does that mean I feel truly alive?

As you can see, each word in the association list is examined through questions related to each other word. This is repeated for the next key word: Place--location. Each word is examined in relation to the others. To "connect" things, you can combine the second and first lists. It is better to go through each one by itself, before you combine them.

This method can help you find the depth in the drops if you picture the Divine as an enormous ocean. Once you have been working with your dreams for a while and are ready to increase awareness and even desire to be aware, it is time for you to start using this method. This is the next step.

This same method can be used to evaluate your thoughts on different aspects of God. What does Siva mean when I say it? What does it mean to say Siva, Buddha, Krishna, Buddha, Jesus, the Virgin Mother Sarasvati Radha, Radha or Kali? This will allow you to see that all of these powers are, in some way, also within yourself.

My goal was to create tools that people can use to accomplish the task. The tools must be used, refined and polished in order to reveal the best results.

PART TWO

MIND, ILLUSION, & WAKING DREAMS

chapter 17

MIND & DREAMS

Why is it necessary to examine the mind to understand dreams? Ask yourself: "Where is the dream happening?" It's the activity of our mind that creates dreams. Although emotions can fire the mind, dreams are not an emotion. The way a dream is presented depends on the state of your mind. How you interpret your dreams will depend on how refined your mind is. Your mental-emotional state determines what and how you do it. It is important to pay attention to what is happening in your head.

We often live our lives as if we are sleeping or as puppies with their eyes just opening. It is important to be careful when confronting our own minds, to avoid becoming overwhelmed by its incredible powers and not being able to manage them. We want to understand how the mind works, what we can expect from it, and how we can improve our mental abilities. Dream Yoga aims to awaken awareness of the mind even when we believe we are asleep.

Dreams are more effective than all our conscious efforts at understanding how the mind works. Mind is the instrument that investigates itself, making it more difficult. Dreams are not conscious manipulation of the mind, so the messages can be more clear. The part of our mind that opposes intuition and wants to destroy it is silenced when we dream. Dreams can help us follow our own path of evolution.

Mind can be either an interpreter or a blocker to Higher Consciousness. If it blocks the way, we can make terrible mistakes that we must pay for, sometimes for as long as twenty-three years, for example, if we marry the wrong person.

Mind is both the creator and interpreter. Eastern teachings call the mind the sixth sense. It interprets the five other senses' input. It interprets emotions, events, and feelings. What does it interpret? It records impressions and stores them in the memory bank. Then it uses them as points for reference. But can we actually perceive the world accurately? How can we remember accurately what we see? Recall is often inaccurate and unreliable, particularly when the senses are out of balance. [29]

What authority do you give to the interpreter? What authority can the mind use to interpret an event or dream in a particular way? How can you ensure that the mind, the interpreter does the job correctly? What are the factors and criteria that influence the interpretation?

It is also important to understand the intelligence and acrobatics that the mind displays. This includes how it constructs things in order to be right, what the mind can do when it feels the need to be someone special, exceptional, or important. It can be misleading if the mind doesn't use discrimination. What are your emotions feeding? What are you giving your mind? What are you listening to? What are you telling it? Your mind's activities in the waking state of consciousness are mostly gossip and based on imagination. Give your mind nourishment. This should be done with intention and willingness. Don't let the Divine shake you awake. It is so different if you are able to awaken by your own choice and desire, rather than having it taken from you.

You will discover how attachments and your lack of awareness create your frustrations, problems, and insecurity. What is the source of attachment? Sensual perceptions are the source of our desires. Attachment is formed when desires are fulfilled. Sometimes, attachment can also occur when a desire is fulfilled. Attachment can lead to passion, anger and delusion, each creating the other. The result is distorted memory and loss discrimination. This self-destructive pattern can be seen and you may realize that the small self must always be lifted above its level in order to become the higher self.

Even if there is a certain level of nonattachment and renunciation, it is important to keep in mind all attachments that still exist. These attachments must also be removed. You will be a slave to the attachments if they aren't. Slavery is your destiny, and you can't get help from anyone else. It is like giving another drink to an alcoholic to cater for your slavish attachments.

One who reinforces their flaws can make you happy and grateful. They will tell you why they need drugs and hate you if they give you the drugs.

To see yourself clearly, you can combine reflection with dreams. This will allow you to understand how to manipulate others subtly. Is it possible to manipulate your dreams? Definitely. Is it possible to end an unfavorable dream? Many of you may have done this. You say, "Oh my gods, I was dreaming!" then you finally wake up thinking, "What an awful dream!" Then, who is it that intervenes and says, “Oh, I should wake up!” What is the observing aspect that can adopt this attitude and take action?

We all have an observer. This observer should be understood. The observer is not an independent entity. It is part of our mind that allows us to be aware. What is it that sees? The mind interprets what the eye sees. How can we see more? We can remove the filters that block out what we don't want to see. We blend the act and the sense of seeing with what is being seen.

The observer is distinct from the part of our minds that creates images and weaves fabrics for its own pleasure and gratification. Each of these areas is responsible for some of our dreams. To be able to deal with the dream material correctly, it is important to identify from which part of our minds we should pay attention.

According to Indian philosophy, Brahma is the Creator. He created endlessly, until he lost all understanding of what he was doing. Have you ever thought that the mind can just keep creating thoughts and thoughts until it doesn't matter what happens. According to mythology, Brahma was confronted by all the gods and told him, "You can’t continue like this." Awareness then comes in and asks, "What’s the point of pouring out an endless stream of thoughts?" You can also see your mind creating sentences and speculating on a future event. It is difficult to understand the mind if you want progress.

Meditating is a way to calm the mind. This is a difficult feat. Before the mind can become still, it takes a lot of practice in watching your mind and eliminating many psychological issues.

Life is always in motion. Even when your awareness is dimmed during sleep, your mind is still in constant motion. You don't know much about the little stimuli that pass through your brain like trains passing through a station. Slowly, the trains of thought move out. Your mind becomes quieter. Just as your eyes adjust when you walk in the dark and you start to see, so too does your awareness of other things as you dream and sleep.

You may not be aware of things you don't normally notice. You might not be able to recall the floor design in the room you work in every day if I asked you. It may be that you only remember it being somewhat light-colored. If you were in complete darkness and could only feel the walls with your fingertips, and there was no light from cars or moonlight, you would be acutely aware that there is a corner and perhaps a door. Your senses are sharpened and you become more alert.

This level of detail perception is also present in your sleep while you're dreaming. What is the difference between when you're awake and when your mind is asleep? Do you think there is a difference?

Although we believe we live in an age of great intellect, technological advancement, we don't know how to communicate with one another. While we can create technological marvels, it is difficult to settle disputes peacefully. We have reached the point where our lack of mental and emotionally discipline can cause the destruction of the world.

The rishis (seers), thousands of years ago, said that the powers of the mind were declining. We will write down the wisdom of ages so that it is not lost." Rishis were people who could perceive intuitively. Their power was so immense that you can read about the "mind-born boys" in Indian mythology. How much have we lost our ability to create with the power and intelligence of the mind?

Slowly, we must find our way back. Slowly, we will discover the power of the mind. Only when we can understand how to realize our dreams, will we be able to truly understand the powers and limitations of the mind. In medieval times, the king had to learn how to read letters. The scribe had power over the king, no matter how large his army was. He had to get that power if he wanted it. You must also acquire mental abilities if you wish to have them.

Although the powers of our minds are vast, many people don't even know they exist. Examine your mind to determine the ability to think, how much energy it uses to think, how it transmits thought into speech, and the power to discriminate and concentrate. The greatest power, and also the easiest to comprehend, is the power of memory. What is the source of your problems? What are the influences that shaped your childhood? Those memories are deeply and strongly ingrained in your memory.

Childhood traumas, such as an accident or the death of a family member, can have a lasting impact on your life later on. This psychological fact is well-known. Some traumas that we have experienced in our lives are so short-lived, they were just a statement made by an authority figure--and thus, they have been forgotten. The statement could have had such an effect on us that their effects can be carried with them throughout our lives if they are not traced back. A single statement, sometimes only minutes or seconds in length, is enough to keep the mind occupied. Because of its strong impact on emotions.

According to the Eastern theory of Reincarnation, these emotional events are anchored in our memories and our emotions. Explore the unconscious. Find out what's there. Many artifacts that were hidden in the earth for thousands of years are being discovered now. Mental things are as resilient as material objects. These memories can be found in our dreams in a more subtle way.

Good recall is key to dreams. Daily reflection and recollection of events can help you improve your memory and observation skills. You must improve your concentration to increase your memory. Otherwise, your thoughts will get distorted and mixed up with others. Your memory can be trained to the extent that you are willing and able to recall where you fell short of your ideals or where you were at the edge. This can be a fascinating study. If you are able to train your memory and have considered the possibility of past lives, then these memories might just start rolling in. The fear and anxiety may be gone. Another possibility is to think "I'm happy that I have enough awareness to escape the problems I created in my life." What if I'm born into another world? "I must be more cautious."

Although the mind can perceive the world, eventually you will be able to see it through another way. In this case, consciousness doesn't need the brain nor the body. This is possible only for those who are able to incorporate a high level of intensity into their spiritual lives. It is essential to first become a loving, warm and well-developed person. If you don't feel called, it is not a good idea to climb the highest mountain. Then you can just do it.

EXERCISES AND REFLECTIONS

1. Mind Watch: Take ten minutes to watch your mind and then write down what you see. This process can be repeated for one hour each day for the next week. You can look over what you write to find the problems and obstacles that drain your energy. Make a color code with different colored highlighters and pencils. Each type of thought (positive, negative or forgetful, inferiority, anger or jealousy) will be given a different color. You can see what is repeating itself and then you will be able to identify what needs to be eradicated. You can also observe the mind to learn more about how it works.

2. What are the characteristics of the mind? You can rank them in order of importance.

3. What mental powers does the mind possess? Make a list. Which mental abilities do you want to improve?

4. Review your dreams. Which dreams are you the observer in? Is it awareness that you are observing or fear?

- 5. These questions will prompt you to reflect on your
- thoughts:How do you think?
- Are you able to think like a pro?
-
- Are you able to see where your dreams come from?
-
-
- Are you aware of where your thoughts originate when you're awake?
-
- What is the point of awareness?

How does it become conscious?

Is it you?

Is it possible to be aware of how much energy you use when you think?

What happens to this energy? What do your thoughts bring?

6. Take note of your own restlessness and see how it affects you. Swami Sivananda told me my first time to contact him many years ago that I should "come home" to India, but only after I could stand motionless for five hours. This practice was very difficult for me, but it allowed me to experience some amazing experiences. This is a must-do exercise because we all have a lot of restlessness. [30] See how long you can remain still for.Restlessness is also a reason why we need constant reassurance. There is always something new in our modern society. It doesn't matter what the Divine does for us: "Oh, that wasn't yesterday." What can I expect from you today? What can I look forward too tomorrow?" Each of us must find the good points in our lives and express gratitude for being given. Why should you accept more help if you don't have gratitude?

chapter 18

CONSCIOUS INFLUENCES

Watch what happens when you wake up to discover how your mind works and how it interferes with the unconscious's messages. Are you able to hear the messages from the unconscious and relay them to your conscious mind? If not, then why not? What does the interaction between mental activities look like? What are the barriers you have put up to prevent the messages from getting through? These messages are important to you?

It is crucial to remember your dreams accurately. Do you think it is neglect or lack of attention? Is it sometimes rejection of the message in the dream? You may sometimes wake up and make a quick assessment to see if you are able to portray the dream. As you write down your dream, you will make small shifts. You might write "I ran away" instead of "I fled," as it sounds more natural. It is likely that you will need to interpret the message later. You will need to consider what you are running from. You can make this type of change with your conscious brain, so why should your subconscious bother to tell you?

This means that you interpret the dream in a particular way so you don't get the message. This is often the case when a dream involves a violent action, such as killing someone. You cannot decide unless you know what you are trying to do. This individual could be a symbol of a trait that needs to be eradicated. For example, greed is a type of monster eating food or attacking innocent children. However, the dream message (I intended to kill him) or the feeling that I might change it should not be changed. . ".") because you are afraid of what others might think. Don't be dependent on what others think. You don't have to share your dreams with anyone.

If you can't face the message of the dream, then you cater to a survival need. This is what you call your ego's need. It is a need to "survive within your own eyes." Physical survival is another. There's survival in the opinion of others. This includes your superiors, colleagues, friends, family members, parents, and children. There is another type of survival: surviving within your own definition of dignity, or surviving in your own terms. Some of our worst traits are too difficult to admit to even ourselves. When we feel compelled, or even tempted, to make ourselves look better, we need to ask "In whose eyes must I survive?". What if this is the ego-sense? This part makes most of our decisions. It could be that our personality parts are competing with each other in fierce, almost insurmountable, competition?

It is amazing, just think about it. What good is it to survive in the eyes and thoughts of the ego? Isn't it more important to live in the Divine Within? Are you willing to ignore the message that is meant to help you? Even though the dream brings a message that is painful, uncomfortable or worrying, it may still be neutral. If understood properly, the dream could actually be a blessing in disguise. If your attitude is right, you may be forced to ask the question "What can I do?" Although you may believe that the dream is pointing out something ugly, without putting the spotlight on it, how would you know it exists? You can choose to end the ugly when you are aware. It will continue to be there for others to see if you don't see it.

You can make your dreams look better by focusing on the fact that you don't just want to look better. Because they are the ones that show me how I can be better, I will listen to my dreams.

You don't have to rely on others' judgments and criticisms about you. Instead, listen to your dreams. You must be able to accept "negative" dreams. Sometimes you might need to pray for courage and ask for clarity in your dreams so that your mind doesn't misinterpret them.

This is an example of a dream I had that wasn't pleasant, but was a blessing.

The Choice Is Yours

One voice told me that you don't need to worry about anything but one thing. That is the only thing that will allow you to attain union with God.

The same voice repeated the words, "Watch out, it's coming now!"

I felt sick and started vomiting. I tried to vomit it out as quickly as possible.

The voice then said, "You cannot say anything that is detrimental to others." This is your old conditioning. You should replace it with a deeper faith. Listening is the best way to learn. It is possible to learn through gentleness or pressure. You have the option to choose.

In my early years, I was so criticised that I started to speak out in self-defense. The dream showed me the problem, which was a blessing. It was clear to me what I needed to do. I was taken back to India by the dream. My Guru said, "You must learn to accept unjust critics and let them go without defending yourself or criticizing the other person."

The most exciting dreams are those that involve undesirable subjects. These dreams show you that you don't have to be ashamed of yourself. We all have to make a decision at some point in our lives. Do we want to live with a bunch of lies and illusions in heaven? This may also be an illusion. Or do we prefer to be honest with ourselves, even if it meant living in hell. You can no longer survive in the eyes or egos of others once you've made this decision.

To be in touch with your soul, you must understand why your conscious mind keeps you from reaching your goals. The mind will play childish (but not childlike, but childish) games as you become more conscious. The mind cannot be diminished continuously by a greater awareness. It is difficult for the Higher Self to communicate with the normal, awake mind. It is impossible. It is impossible. The ignorant ego doesn't know how to handle it, and then becomes extremely silly. This is similar to being in a trauma situation. You want to laugh at the situation or find a way to get out. Listening to your Higher Self is a way to keep yourself from getting too excited. Take a look at what comes from the unconscious first.

Your ego could play dangerous tricks. If it is really in your dreams, it could manipulate your dreams to project its agenda into your subconscious. This can be hard if you don't take the time to study your unconscious and learn the language it uses. Once you are as conscious as possible of the entire unconscious spectrum, you will be able to spot the tricks. You must look at the whole spectrum of creative aspects of your mind. It is important to not start meditation too soon. You cannot tell if you are hallucinating, daydreaming, or really connecting with the creative spirit within.

It is possible to dream you are a great priestess. Then you wake up one day and tell everyone that you were a great priestess in your past lives. However, if you continue living your life and not being affected by the dream, it may be a manifestation of your ego. You may not want to share the dream if you are genuinely convinced that it has a spiritual meaning. This is your secret. At the very least, you will observe yourself and try to figure out how you can live up your dream. You might share the dream with someone you trust. If you don't make any changes in your life, then you are not taking the dream seriously.

If you are sincere, and don't make any mistakes in your interpretations, your dreams will reveal the truth in a very gentle manner. They will tell you.

In self-help groups, you may have noticed how much admiration is given to the person who is brave. Not to the one who avoids the question but to the one that recognizes the insight. Everyone can see a weakness or shortcoming and everyone admires the one who does.

Who in your life creates situations that you cannot accept? Who makes the judgments? One or two or three personality elements are the ones who say "No!" You need to think about the power you have given your personality aspects. You should remove this power as soon as possible. It is like giving someone a very difficult job. This is not something you would do in a business setting. This personality aspect should be viewed in the same manner. You can evaluate its performance and warn it about the consequences if it doesn't change. If necessary, you can fire it just like any other incompetent employee. Put it back in its place.

Sit in the judgement seat.

A sixty-three year-old woman was one of my students. She said that she wouldn't talk about dreams any more. She couldn't interpret dreams and was so bad that she couldn't even admit to it.

I replied, "I don't recall anything from our dream workshops that you have to be so insistent about."

After a week of convincing, she finally came up with the disturbing dream. She had a dream that she visited a beautiful church and met the Pope. She fell in love with the Pope. She began to cry because she was so upset. "Now, do you understand what I mean about how terrible it was?"

I am?"

I said, "Wait a minute. What is your idea of closeness? What is your concept of oneness? How do you define love?

She understood intimacy, closeness and love when she was surrounded by a man and woman.

"What does Pope mean?"

"The Pope is a representative for the Divine on Earth."

I asked her: "Were there any sexual feelings that were associated with the dream?"

"No, it's just warmth and gentleness. It is a feeling of being close to someone, but not sexual contact.

"Now what are you worried about?"

"I woke up!" However, if I hadn't, it could have been sinful! What then?

I told her that even in your wildest moments, your mind wouldn't allow you to picture yourself in an embrace of Jesus. The Pope is the next best symbol for union with God because he's at least human." I sensed that she would soon be in an embrace of the Divine in some way. "What the dream reveals is that this oneness will take place in your lifetime--if it is not sooner, then at time of you death." I then told her several dreams of mine to help explain the symbolism better. She was relieved.

She was able to forget all her worries and revert back to her former self. With serious intentions to return and take up residency, she left the Ashram. For six months, I didn't hear from her. Finally, I called her office to find out that she had suffered a stroke when she returned from work that left her paralysed from the waist down. Because she couldn't understand me, she was unable to talk and became very agitated. However, her hearing was normal so I was able speak with her. Here's what I said: "The Pope was the symbol that God will hold you in His arms." There is nothing to be worried about." She was gone in a couple of months.

POSITIVE USE OF THE CONSCIOUS MIND

Ask yourself: "Can I manage to suspend all judgement?" This is important both on the dream and conscious levels. You will not be forgiving of others and you will make the same mistakes yourself at the end. This is the Last Judgment. Learn to be more understanding and compassionate and to control your immediate reactions, objections, and criticisms.

It is important to do your own research. To overcome preconceived notions and self-imposed limitations that can hinder your research, brainstorm your thoughts of mind and consciousness. Self-investigation requires courage, honesty, and sincerity. How can you conduct your own research? Ask yourself questions like "Can I manage to suspend all judgement?" This is just one question. There are many others. The next question you should ask is, "How can I manage my anxiety?" How about my mental and emotional security? What can I do to alter my comfortable and familiar picture of the world meaning your personal world.

Ask yourself: "Am I ready to travel the uncharted waters of the unconscious?" This is what we do when researching ourselves--we chart those seas. We want to find out what's there. This is risky work. We need to find out where the undercurrents are and where the rifts and the cliffs are below the surface.

Ask yourself, "How can I manage my anxiety?" How will my mental perceptions change if I expect that certain phenomena, such as prophetic dreams, have a basis in reality?

One psychiatrist I met in a big city said to me, "You know, after your last visit, I had an amazing and clear dream about your ashram." Are there any guest lodges, small offices, bookstores, or old houses where you can eat your meals?

I said, “Yes, exactly.”

He continued to describe the grounds, and then asked: "And is there any young man there with particularly big blue eyes?" He also provided details about the man's appearance.

"Yes. "Yes.

He finally came, and as we walked around the Ashram together, he pointed to landmarks that he had seen from his own experience. A young man with large blue eyes came by and said "That's him, that's the one!"

"I saw in my dream."

The psychiatrist was then afraid. The psychiatrist had to accept the dream experience because it was confirmed by his visit. However, he didn't want to accept it. Fear! Fear! Fear! Fear! Fear! After signing up for a ten-day stay at the Ashram, he left and went to a motel further down the road. He couldn't take it anymore.

You need to ask yourself: "How can I change my familiar and comfortable view of the world?" There are no phenomena, because there is not empirical evidence for any. There is a lot of evidence that exists outside our social, educational, and racial contexts, which we have never gathered.

Technological men will tell you, "Yes, it's possible to build rockets." We can reach the moon, and soon we will be able to go to Saturn and Mars." If we are able to build complex devices that can lift us out of the gravitational fields, what symbolically can we do to take us beyond our own mental gravitational fields? Is it not possible to imagine that the mind can make equipment on the physical level to overcome the greater forces of outer space? The mind can create anything it wants.

Scientists have a clear understanding of the barriers that surround the Earth's surface: gravity, electromagnetic fields, Van Allen belts, etc. What are the mental barriers that stop awareness expanding? Awareness must use all the extra power that the mind normally expends on its own barriers. What forces are similar to gravity? They push you down and pull your back to the smallest atmosphere. Ballast is what prevents you from taking flight: Fear, survival, desire, and mental background noises.

They prevent the unconscious messages from getting through.

It is difficult for the Higher Self to start a process of clarification if you are too focused on yourself or limited in what is possible. You can gain more insight if you let go of the residue in your mind. This will result in greater awareness, which is the hallmark of consciousness. Only then can a broad range of mental abilities be realized.

EXERCISES AND REFLECTIONS

1. Pay attention to your own tendency to alter a dream while you write it down. Notice where it hurts to see the truth. Ask yourself: "Would it be better to hold on to the illusion of a better view about myself than to face

the truth?" If you refuse to listen, the facts will be presented in a less gentle manner. You can cooperate with your own evolution by working with your dreams.

2. Make a copy of your dream and write it down exactly as it is. You can later divide your dreams into positive and negative. Seeing that you have enough positive material will help you to not try to fool yourself to survive,.

3. What does "surviving in your own eyes" mean for you? What are you going to do to survive emotionally?

4. Write down a vivid and exciting dream. Sign your name and date the dream. Then seal the envelope by sealing it. Write down what you remember about the dream one month later. Find out what your memory has changed by opening the envelope.

5. There is a way to understand why certain situations occur in your life. Write down briefly the events of Monday night. Place the paper in a sealed envelope and add the date. The process can be repeated on Tuesday, Wednesday and Thursday. Write down the entire week's events on Sunday. Open the envelopes to find out what you forgot, what you misunderstood, and what you did differently. You can extend the time by two weeks and then write down everything you remember about those two weeks. You can extend this time to two months, three or more months, and then again, write down all you remember from those two weeks. You will be amazed at how sharpening one's memory can change your dreams if you also record them.This requires a lot of effort. It is a difficult task, but it will help you learn more about yourself, your mistakes, and the factors that have led to your current life. You'll see the areas where you could have made better decisions. You will eventually be able recall every event in your past if you put the effort. You will eventually be able recall past events after two years.

6. Ask yourself these questions:

- How reliable is my memory?
- What is your perception of me?
-
- What can my senses do to alter and twist facts?

Who or what makes the changes in my memories of events?

7. Ask yourself:

- Can I bring myself to keep all judgment suspended?
- Are you willing to explore the unknown waters of the unconscious?
-
- What can I do to deal with my anxiety?
-

What can I do to ensure my mental and/or emotional safety?

What can I do to challenge my worldview?

- What are the barriers of mind that prevent awareness from expanding?

chapter 19

THE UNCONSCIOUS IN DAILY LIFE

In our research of dreams, we have seen how the unconscious can communicate its messages through dreams. Now we will examine how the conscious can influence these messages. But can the unconscious influence our waking lives as well?

Is it possible to live purely by logic and reason? These qualities are often referred to as the best attributes of the mind in the West. But is this true? While logic and reason are great at creating things, we need to understand the power of intuition and how it can create new things. The symbols we see in our waking lives can be interpreted as dreams. What grabs our attention? The unconscious directs our eyes.

What do you see when you open your eyes for the first time in the morning? What do you see? Are you concerned about time? Did you ever think about time? Find out. Do you feel attracted to brightly colored flowers? You might need to be more subtle if you find yourself attracted to flowers in beautiful amethyst colors. Is it your health if you are attracted to healthy green plants? What is your growth? Are you a plant-lover who is not happy with the appearance of the plant?

You can reflect your mood by choosing what clothes you wear when you get up from your chair. What should you wear today, and what should you avoid? You can wear a white shirt or a pale yellow shirt with long sleeves and short sleeves. What is festive? Simple? You want something simple? What kind of belt do you use? Are you ready to loosen up? Are you looking to improve your self-esteem? Do you find yourself constantly blaming yourself for self-reproach?

Your state of mind often depends on what your eyes see in your home. One day you may be focusing on all the windows and doors, but then suddenly one door opens up and you start to wonder why. You might not be allowed to go through that door. Your sense of observation improves and you can pick up cues from your actions. You will eventually realize that your dreams are not the only thing you can rely on.

If your gaze is constantly returning to the phone, you might want to stop and ask "Is there anyone I should call?" This does not necessarily mean you should call that person. However, it may be that you should write or communicate another way. We will use more of the intuitive ability that scientists have identified as our brain's one-fifth. What about the remaining four-fifths of our brain? It would be great to be able to access even the fifth, instead of only having a small fraction of our mental abilities?

If you notice something that is pleasing to your eyes, it could be a sign of the way you are thinking. If you continue to notice the undesirable or unpleasant, it is likely that this is the result of your unconscious. Your hidden desires will be revealed as you begin to observe yourself. You will begin to understand yourself better.

I was once asked by a woman why people would buy artificial flowers. It's horrible! Flowers are now artificial! "What else is going to become artificial in our daily lives?"

When I visited her house, I noticed a lovely arrangement of flowers. It was an artificial arrangement, which I discovered when I got closer to see it. "Why did your mind change?" I asked.

"I don't really understand. After all that I've told you and everyone else, it's hypocritical. They are just too expensive.

I replied, "Well, let us sit down and enjoy a cup de tea." Perhaps we will find out.

It was evident to me. It was obvious to me that she was going through a difficult time in her life. She was going through a divorce and felt no joy or color. These artificial flowers were a great way to bring joy, color, and brightness into her life. They could be kept for as long as she needed and she could get rid of them whenever she wanted. It was not like her marriage had ended. I was shown that when we want to find balance in our lives, it is possible to do so by using very unusual means, even against our very strong convictions.

Symbolism is important because it allows us to see the whole truth when we are trying to survive and accept ourselves. It would be too difficult. But, if we don't get to know ourselves, then we will blame others for our mistakes, oversights, and negligence. The ego can't take criticism. The soul also cries. Sometimes, we don't know why we cry. If we keep putting our inner self down and hurting it, we might one day extinguish the inner Light. It will be through our actions.

One of Germany's most well-known psychiatrists was a friend of my father. I was often invited to his office as a child to have dinner with him. Sometimes I had to wait for a very long time. One time, I was waiting in the waiting area when a patient was also waiting. The man noticed that I had brought lots and lots of pencils and paper with me. He asked if he could borrow them. He began to draw. He looked at his paper and looked at me when the nurse arrived. I kept the paper. Later that evening, at the dinner table I asked the psychiatrist: "What did this man say to you?"

He replied, "Oh, it's not for me to know. But why would you want to ask?

I said, "I think that he's going shoot himself."

"Why would you believe that?"

I showed it to him. I pointed out the gun to him, but he couldn't see it.

He was more attentive to the words of his patients as a psychiatrist. He began to pay more attention to the unconscious messages after this incident. He tried out different methods, asking me to bring paper and pencils and inviting me to spend an hour in the waiting area. He would sometimes come into the house to ask Sylvia what he thought of the picture.

The unconscious can give us clues about our own lives and those of others. It is up to us to discover what it says. Because the conscious mind is so busy, always distracted, and often distracted, the unconscious provides clues. It is amazing how much you live by metaphor and symbol. It will surprise you to discover that the unconscious controls your everyday life.

It is important to understand our inner selves. Sometimes, we can look outside to see our inner qualities. You are likely to compare yourself with others and be competitive if you constantly try to make others look better. Although you can make people look good with your jewelry, watches and clothes, it is only temporary. You can impress people with your clothes, jewelry and watches temporarily. But once you start to reveal more about yourself--perhaps in the second or subsequent meeting--the advertisement image fades. People ask: "What's the truth?" It is a lie. Those who project a false image are only fooling themselves for a short time. It eventually leaves behind an accumulation of bad actions and attitudes, which can interfere with their true desires and goals.

Be helpful if you want people to view you as helpful.

Find out what it means for you to be a friend. You will then be known for who you are. You will become real. People will no longer see through your image and you won't have to worry about what happens after the show ends. The effect of a show only lasts so long. When I think back to how many premieres I've seen and the big shows that I've seen, I can't recall any.

However, I do recall a teacher who was warm and helpful.

Many men who were prisoners of war told me what they had done to sustain themselves. It was an image of someone who had been a good person in their life, such as a teacher, professor, or clerk at the corner shop. It wasn't someone who had made a fireworks image. A flash that goes out quickly is not what it was. We don't remember those images so why bother building more? All of us want something that lasts. We need to take the time to reflect on what we are good at and work towards it. This will allow us to live in harmony, peace, and less anxiety.

Our lives will be richer and more meaningful if we allow ourselves to be more affected by our symbolic messages. For example, if a woman notices that her posture isn't straightening out, she can ask herself these questions: "Am I not taking a position?" Can I not stand for myself? Do I feel weighed down by some burden? It is important to ask yourself, "What is it?" She is more comfortable with this process than when someone else says, "Look. You are like this or this, and these is the changes that you must make," she would likely feel insulted and harshly treated.

Take the time to research. You can learn more from your own experience by paying attention to symbol, image, and metaphor. Your inner guide will give you more guidance the more you pay attention to them. You will soon discover that your inner guide is not only a teacher or guru, but also a friend who is happy to help you if you allow it.

Beautiful photos of Jesus knocking at a door without a handle are available. This image communicates that the door must be opened from the inside.

Clarify what you mean when you say "symbol" or "image". Can you interchange the two words? If you see a beautiful picture of a Buddha, does it make the image different than the Buddha as a symbol. What is the Buddha's symbol status? Could the Buddha be a symbol for a particular religion? People might be seen prostrating in front of the image. This could make you think "What strange behavior!" They do this because the Buddha is an object to them, a piece carved wood or stone. The image of Buddha to a trained Buddhist is however a symbol for the state beyond the mind.

The Christian teachings refer to Jesus as the Son, Messiah, Good Shepherd, Son of God, and Lamb of God. He is also the healer, teacher, carpenter, and the Messiah. Although we may speak of Jesus in different ways, it is always the exact same person. How can we make Jesus a symbol of Higher Consciousness, or Christ Consciousness, in our minds? We need to clarify the words that we use to symbolise Higher Consciousness. This is because we create confusion in our minds.

The Kundalini chakras are also not images. [32] They symbolize the exercises needed to fully understand each level of consciousness.

Is Radha and Krishna an image or a symbol when we look at the picture? It's both. Because human beings cannot understand the Divine, or the Cosmic Energy in its entirety, Krishna is within a human body. To show that he's not a normal human being, the color blue is used. This indicates the vastness and infiniteness of the sky. We humans desire something greater than ourselves so we can picture the Divine as this. Radha, the symbol of Creation, is another aspect. In Hinduism, the female aspect of Buddhism is used to symbolize Creation. This is because during pregnancy and birth, a woman's ability is obvious while her paternity is not. Radha is the Creative Force that manifests, and all that has come into being. Radha and Krishna love Radha, which symbolizes the Cosmic Forces embracing Creation, and Creation loving the Cosmic Forces.

You can also look at the images and symbols that you have embedded in your life, and how they affect you today. What does your mother and father symbolically mean? It is easy to forget the things we put into our young minds. Many times, the problems that we face in our professional and personal lives later on are linked to those childhood images. Your father may have been too busy to play with your child and your mother told him to punish David.

These old images cannot be allowed to cling on to you as a mature man or woman. These images are drains that can rob you your energy. It is important to examine the remnants of these symbols and images that are still lingering within your head. Once you understand that your parents made the best decision, even if it wasn't always the right one, you will be able to free yourself and them.

You had no idea what kind of world was waiting for you when you entered the world through your mother's womb. You can't know what your spiritual life will look like until you are there. A North American Indian tribe used a ritual called "Ring of Fire" to symbolize this journey into the unknown. The ground was lit by a ring of fire that symbolized knowledge. To be able to cross the fire and reach the center of knowledge, you must have the courage. You have to be brave to go in because you never know what you'll find.

EXERCISES AND REFLECTIONS

1. Use examples from your own life to help you define your terms "symbol", "image". Begin with your family. Start with your family. Which image do you still hold of your father? Your father was the ruler of your house. He was the judge. Was he the punisher? He was the provider. Who was the

caregiver? He was the financier. Did he build your life in the context of the family? He was the one who destroyed? Perhaps he was the destroyer?

2. Next, look at your mother. Your mother was your comforter, your food when you were little. Did she also teach you as a child? Did she serve as your teacher and also your disciplinarian Could she have created and destroyed hopes? Maybe she was a source for pleasure. Maybe she appeared enormous, almost like a goddess. Little children see the mother and father as a god and goddess of unmeasurable power.

3. Look at yourself after thinking about the symbols and images of your family. Take a look at yourself in a mirror. You may be wearing different clothes or not. Which image are you trying to project? Is your body a good image? Do you consider your body a symbol of something? What is your body a symbol? Indulgence? Harshness? How can you live a healthy life? The body can be read like a book.

4. Take a look at yourself in the mirror. What does your face say? It can be kind or resentful?

5. Listening to your thoughts is another way to learn about your thinking.

6. You can increase your creativity and enhance your life by incorporating symbol and metaphor into your daily life. You can add symbolic meaning to your day by incorporating symbolism into your everyday work. While washing dishes, think about how you can bring symbolic meaning to your daily work. [33] Purify your mind by washing your car. Clearing out old ideas and clutter from your head is a good way to clear your yard. You don't have to be open to criticism from others by doing this work.

7. People find it difficult to listen in a normal state of consciousness. People rarely listen to their own thoughts and even less to others. Ever wonder why all the goddesses and gods wear beautiful earrings? Precious is the ear that listens. What else can you do to show an ear is precious?You can hit someone with your fist, or you can hold them gently. To symbolize the precious hand that can heal, the goddess might wear a bracelet made of lotuses.

Nowadays, jewelry can be worn as body ornamentation. Jewelry is no longer a symbol of preciousness. You can still use your jewelry as a symbol of your intentions: necklaces to show your desire to transform self-will into Divine will; earrings for the precious ear which hears; bracelets or rings to represent the hand that can reach out and touch with compassion; and bracelets or rings to remind you that your jewelry is precious.

chapter 20

WAKING DREAMS

Both daydreams and night dreams are made from the same substance. They get their power from the mind. It is important to examine our thoughts, which are often not in our control. Otherwise they could run amok and take over our lives. To understand ourselves, it is necessary to examine the images that travel through our minds, particularly images that are triggered by emotions. Examine them carefully and examine them closely to discover what effects they have.

What is the difference between dreaming while you sleep and daydreaming? There are many dreams that we have in our waking state. The mind can interfere with perception and cause it to take us in different directions. Each person tries to convey an image to another, but the images are interpreted differently by other minds. We don't know if we succeed or fail. Each mind creates its own scripts, with its own dreams qualities, such as beautiful woman, ugly women, good man or bad man, or threatening person. However, none of these may be correct. It is important to accept the facts as they actually are.

A president of one of the best universities visited me years ago and was extremely upset. He had previously met with a couple from lower-middle class who were asking questions about the university. He treated them harshly. He found out later that the insignificant and lowly-looking people had been willing to donate two million dollars for his university. But they decided to give it to another university. He was furious. I asked him, "Does everyone with a IQ of 150 wear glasses with horn-rimmed lenses?" These stereotypes are created to show how a rich person, an intellectual, or a doctor looks.

There is no limit to what you can do in the spiritual realm. There will be twenty images of the spiritual leader to which twenty people can relate. As a sanyasin, I knew early on that I could not play these kinds of games. I would have preferred to be a dancer in the theater. I don't see why I would give up my comfortable life just to continue playing the same game?

One person may project a threatening image on another. What makes someone more dangerous than another? It increases their self-worth. They are saying, "Look at what I can do to deal with such an intimidating individual!".

Sometimes you might think you're being intuitive, but you could be acting from your past conditioning. You may be suspicious of someone, but this suspicion could result from the law on thought association

Their red hair and green eyes make you think of someone who has disappointed or treated you badly, so you subconsciously fear that they will do the exact same. This kind of oversimplification is not something you can afford. The law of thought association must be understood in the context of your life.

You will be amazed at how difficult it can be to grasp new experiences on your own. They can always be seen in the light that comes from old experiences. We are constantly influenced by the color of a person's hair. If we form strong opinions, we can judge others uncritically. It is possible to believe that people who wear glasses cannot see what is in front of them. We then operate on this assumption.

Many people perceive things incorrectly. It can be very difficult to see clearly. While you may be able to see clearly in certain areas, it is very difficult to see in others.

Even more challenging is the fact that you don't know where your blind spots are.

Here's an example. Let's say that there is an Oriental rug hanging on a wall. It is too far away for us to see it. It might be a very interesting wallpaper with a medallion at the center. It could be that you think it's a carpet with a central medallion, which is hung on a wall. I believe the design is wallpaper. We could argue endlessly without ever getting anywhere. You might wonder if your perception of wallpaper is correct if someone else says so. It might be possible to agree with three others that wallpaper is indeed wallpaper if you hear them all.

This is brainwashing. It is brainwashing. You may experience this throughout your entire life until you no longer accept your own perceptions. It's easy to follow the crowd, and believe what is told you.

You don't need to question or investigate if you believe. If you truly want to find out, however, you will put in the effort to research and discover.

Advertising exploits ignorance to great advantage. It tells you something is good for your health or even better than the competitor's product and you should buy it. This is what we can call hypnosis. You may eat foods that are not good for you or apply creams to your skin that you don't really need if you are sufficiently hypnotized.

Our entire way of living is conditioned. It will be difficult to accept the contrary of what you believe. You might cry or feel upset. It is easy to believe that something is true, even though you don't know the truth. All of our problems are the result of past conditioning. The mind behaves like a computer programmed to do certain things. When you ask it to change the program, it doesn't know how.

Let's take religion as an example. Let's say you believe what you have been told, and that Jesus is the only way to salvation and eternal life. When you go to university, you will find that scholars debate whether historical evidence supports Jesus' existence. You will feel a change in your belief system that you had programmed into your brain. Because you have lived with this belief, it may seem like your entire life has been thrown out of balance. What can you do now?

You may be able to intellectually solve the problem, or you might give up on Jesus Christ and accept another belief. You may be tempted to give up on Jesus and accept a belief that is not supported by historical evidence. Instead of allowing your beliefs to drive your thinking, you can get out of them. It is possible to say, "It sounds intriguing and possible, but it is not true."

You can tune into the Christ Consciousness of Jesus, regardless of whether there was a historical Jesus. This can be done by repeating the Lord's Prayer five times per day or by memorizing the Sermon On the Mount and repeating it aloud to yourself. You will learn a new kind of knowledge through experience.

Your unconscious can give you direction where your rational, conscious mind can't. It may take some time to believe certain things, but you will eventually discover for yourself. Only you can experience it.

Examine your thinking process. Discover how your mind constructs its own picture using partial facts. Let's say you are looking at a microphone and don't know much about how it works. Your imagination might take what you know and create something completely new. One might think, "There's a complicated connection of wires that hear sound. Vibration travels along these wires and is then decoded." . . "You may present your guesswork so confidently that it seems as if you actually know. This is something we do quite often. We do this often when we don't have all the facts. This information is not reality. This information is just a fabrication of our minds using very small fragments.

If I'm not familiar with someone, or if I don't know their thoughts, I can draw conclusions. This is often done unconsciously. I could think to myself, "Well this young man wears glasses and dark pants with a white shirt." He seems very neat so it is likely that he is decent and hardworking. He must be a worker in an office. I am sure he is intelligent." I then think I have a good idea of what this guy is like and how he behaves. But how do I get there? My creativity is largely driven by fragments of facts.

My mind will weave in the opinions and perceptions of others if they come to me. My imagination is what creates my entire picture of him. He may then think that she doesn't really know me if I meet him. If I already know what kind of person he's, I will not let her get to understand me. He becomes my rival and I may never see him as a person I imagined.

Life is complex. Understanding this will help us to be more understanding and compassionate with one another. We also know that misunderstandings can occur at any time. The mind can weave endless fabrics using any amount of thread or material it can find. Are those weavings true? No. You cannot make yourself truly known if I don't allow you to. It is an illusion I create and harbour.

> Sometimes, we believe that God is a myth. Once you have a good idea about God, it is easy to forget.

If you think about the energy that you call God, it is a concept. It's like a concept about a person. This concept is God's opponent in your mind. This is your illusion.

All powers of the mind include daydreaming, fantasy, and hallucination. The skillful or unskilled use of imagination is what is really being referred to.

Daydreams are a string of images without a specific purpose or goal. They are not driven by the fire of emotions or the desire to create. I can dream that I am the most beautiful or intelligent woman in the world. The mind can drift if we don't do anything about our dreams. This causes us to lose a lot energy.

Daydreaming creates a fantasy world for us to live in and a fantasy picture of ourselves. We make fantasy after fantasy about others until we are confronted with something that is unpleasant and then we wake up to realize, "Oh, this was not what I expected." This is because we don't have the courage to see the truth.

Maybe you created a fantasy of being together. You believed in a love that didn't really exist. Because you believed in the fantasy, you didn't care about investigating whether it actually existed. Then, your marriage ends and you wake up to the reality. These are the facts. You may have built a world all your own after twenty- or thirty years of marriage. This world crumbles when your spouse leaves.

Yoga is a practice that lays the foundation for our ability to see the world slowly and steadily. The act of seeing. And what is seen.[34] Does it have any reality? Or are you merely seeing the fantasies of your mental imaginations? Sometimes you might be able give life to a fantasy. But how long? The fantasy you create is only possible because of your own abilities. If you stop empowering it the fantasy will collapse.

What are we feeding our minds? It is vital to understand. What are our fantasies? Many people in psychiatric units create fantasies that they believe are real. Hallucinations can be described as a stronger form of fantasy in which imagination and emotions are uncontrolled and are able to overcome reason.

When my Guru predicted the problems I would face in the West upon my return, he said that "I see dark clouds gathering" and my mind could make the most destructive, dramatic, and powerful dream from his words. You can create or contribute to the situation if you are willing to sit with it for long enough. Negative daydreams, such as depression can lead to sickness. Sometimes our powerful minds can prevent us from changing or creating a better script. If we are subject to negative criticism, our dignity, reputation, or self-worth, and we accept it as true, we can be a weak and worthless person and view ourselves in that light.

Each of us has our own dreams. Our dreams may include a dream home or the discovery of a cure for cancer. There are many motivations for our dreams, from personal glory and financial gain to great compassion.

Sometimes, it's a mix of all three. Because it all begins as a dream, we don't anticipate the many stages that will be required to make the dream a reality. This would disrupt the dream's perfection. We feel pain when our dreams don't come true in our real lives. This pain can be seen as self-created from a yogic perspective.

Psychologists often invite me to attend their workshops and I am always happy to discuss them with them. One such workshop saw a woman break down and cry. People gathered around her and patted her shoulder and said, "Don't cry. We all love and cherish you. There's no need to weep.

The psychologist noticed that I was feeling very uneasy about this and suggested that we work together.

"You want to tell something."

I replied, "Yes." This is the greatest lie. Your gestures are dishonest under these circumstances. The woman is truly in pain and everyone has promised her their love. What happens to your love if she brings her two children to you and asks, "Can I stay here until my job is found?" You are selfishly trying to make yourself feel better, but it doesn't have a grain of truth. It is a fantasy. We make a world out of nothing, and then we make it real for others.

We also believe in the reality and meaning of our existence so strongly that we don't want to see death. If we do, it may not be so different than moving from one room into another. We move from one dimension into another at death. There is no reason to be afraid.

It is amazing how powerful it is to think up and create things! It is powerful. Every man and woman carries the image of a dream lover. [35] Although this is a different type of dream, we must recognize its existence. The dream lover for a woman is tall and beautiful. He does the right thing at just the right moment. He is a wonderful protector, a romantic and a great lover. He may have enough money, or be very wealthy. When she meets a man, she compares his characteristics to her list of dream lovers. Men do the exact same. Who can match up? It is impossible to see the dream lover image in reality. Is there such a person?

Dreams do not transform the spouse or husband. The dream also does not bring the dream lover into our lives. Trouble is when the dream partner's image doesn't match the reality. We cannot create the dream partner directly. However, we can make ourselves into someone else and create a person who is not worthy of the dream lover. This creates feelings and insecurity as well as worthlessness. Many women try to manipulate their husbands into becoming the man they want after getting married. He isn't the dream lover. There is always an edge.

There is no perfect relationship. Even the ideal relationship we imagine isn't perfect. Even if we're married, we feel disappointed and lonely. This is why we feel lonely and hurt. We try to overcome this feeling. We are born and die alone. What do we have in common? While we can all share some material, what happens inside of us is entirely ours. Each person interprets things in their own way. Many people dream of a perfect relationship, but it is impossible to make a reality. It is impossible to expect something. What are you going to do? You can either force the issue to make your dream a reality, or accept the fact that other dreamers may have different dreams. Although two people might temporarily dream the exact same thing because they share the same desires and goals, their lives will change once their desires have been fulfilled.

We see a young couple running together through a field in TV and movie advertising. They are focusing on the sun at this stage in their relationship. We cannot live in paradise forever. You have to rethink what you see when you turn forty years old or fifty years. Why? Because you are mature. You are able to see beyond your imagination and the horizon. You can see both the light and shadow, and you learn to accept them both.

People have romantic fantasies about their past lives. One woman believed she was Queen Mumtaz for whom the Taj Mahal was constructed, but she didn't realize it was a tomb and not a castle. She was a normal housewife who wanted the opportunity to be someone. Do something if you want to become somebody. Study, learn, practice and acquire a skill. Become unique. However, fantasy and daydreaming won't make you unique. People will see you as someone who is caught up in illusions.

Daydreams can cause great difficulties because of the immense power of illusion. Because they want to be accepted and recognized, some people don't recognize the illusions as what they really are. It is essential to discriminate. After you've experienced enough pain and disappointment, it becomes clear that you have lived with illusion. You are continually disappointed in yourself and hurt by your pride.

Realize how much energy you are wasting on your desires, illusions and emotions and shift your focus to higher consciousness. Many people don't even realize that such a deal exists. You will eventually see the truth of what you do to yourself through pain and disappointment. It could take thousands of lifetimes, one hundred thousand lives, or a million lifetimes. It is too expensive. Do it now.

EXERCISES AND REFLECTIONS

1. These "dreams" can be used to help you daydream or dream in the waking state. Write them down and then take out the key words, just like with nighttime dreams.

2. You can also take a situation in daily life—especially an emotionallycharged one—and look at it as if it were a dream.

   - What is the setting?
   - Who are the characters?
   - What is the action?
   - What is your position as the *I* in the dream?
   - Which *I* is it?
   - What is the resolution, or the question you are left with?

3. Look at all the expectations that you have, even in conver-sations withother people, as dreaming in the waking state.

4. Examine your sense perceptions.

    - Do you know which of your senses are dominant and which less developed?
    - Are any of your senses in competition? For example, if a person appears pleasant to your eyes but sounds terrible to your ears, you may reject him or her because your sense of hearing overrules sight. You may even think you are making a wise judgement based on logic and reason, or intuitive perception. Find out how this applies in your life.
    - When you make snap decisions, how much are your sense perceptions responsible?
    - How reliable are they?

5. Try listening to a person while you are doing some handiwork. You willreally hear what the individual says. If you look up at the person, you hear only half of what they are saying because the face very often conveys a different message from the voice. When these two messages are conflicting, communication is off-key.

6. Review your dreams and find out which senses are active in your dreams.If you can bring all five senses into your dreams and recall their involvement, you will sharpen your sense perceptions in waking life. This will have a big impact on your life because we experience life through our senses.

7. Cultivate the senses by paying attention to how they operate. Spend a weekinvestigating one sense. You may become aware that you have just scratched the surface.[36]

8. Try answering these questions:

    - What is the power of perception?
    - Is the power of perception on the mental level?
    - Is the power of perception intuitive?

- Is the power of perception sensual?
- Is the power of perception the same or different if it is intellectual or intuitive? Is it separate?
- How can you assess the power of your perception?
- How can you become aware if your power of perception expands?
- Does it mean you have greater understanding?
- Is the understanding more a knowing of the heart or a knowing of the mind?

9. Find out where your past experiences interfere with clear perception.

- How do you unconsciously apply the laws of thought association in your daily life?
- In how many different areas does it come up?
- Do you use this power beneficially?
- Does it always undermine your own security?

10. Ask yourself:

- What is a dream?
- Who is the dreamer?

chapter 21

DIRECTING THE POWER

Instead of being caught in illusion, you can use the same power of imagination to create something worthwhile. One way to do this is through creative visualization. If you feel very unhappy, yet you are not at the point of being able to deal with your problems directly, I can say: “Sit down, relax, close your eyes, and let me take you into a world of fantasy. Let us go into a beautiful garden where you can hear the gentle sounds of a brook, and see an array of flowers and birds.” When your imagination becomes involved, you can continue to explore and complete this picture. In this way you can change a negative, destructive mood into a positive one.[37] The problem that created the despair will not necessarily go away, but you can at least temporarily release pressure from the nervous system and the emotions. Then in the same way that I led you into the fantasy, I can perhaps point out that what you despair over is only a different fantasy, a different dream.

To develop a positive use of imagination, the mind has to be given direction. If I want to invent something, I have to put my desires and imagination into focus and give them a boost from my emotions. Then I can be creative and bring my dream into fruition. If a daydream is just the fantasy of the ego wanting to be somebody special, nothing much will happen. Creativity requires the use of will—taking action. The difference between the artist and the daydreamer is that something will emerge from the daydream of the artist, while the person who is egocentric and thinks of himself as a hero, or thinks of herself as the most beautiful woman in the world, achieves nothing beneficial. It remains an illusion that is bound to get shattered.

We have to recognize that one of the driving forces behind our nightdreams, daydreams and illusions, is desire. We scheme to fulfill those desires and spend most of our lives in the attempt. From this thought process or dreaming we begin to act. Some people act quickly, and for those with powerful emotions the actions are compulsive. But if you are sincere, the Divine will also create the circumstances to fulfill your good desires if they benefit other people as well. My Guru said, "Dream that you are a saint and you will become one." But then you have to put your dream into action; you have to think like a saint. He said to me, "Think of yourself always as Radha, and nothing is impossible." The Bible says the same—if we have faith, we can move mountains, we can do what seems impossible.

Desire creates, or is the instigator that creates, the images in the mind. When we visualize the image strongly and clearly, we work to bring it into manifestation. If you want to manifest your dreams, go through the creative process in your own mind. You need both your dream and the desire to manifest it. Then you can bring your chosen path to fulfillment. Sometimes you have to cut back a bit on the grandness of your dream to make it possible. If your expectations are too high, they are often of the ego. You already know that you will never achieve them because they are beyond the human capacity to achieve, so you have created a beautiful excuse. If your wishful thinking is wonderful—great. Keep it. But you must not deceive yourself into believing that the wish is already a reality in your life. The dream may be showing you what you can become, but you may not be there yet.

If your goal is to be a success in business, and if you put in the effort, which might include more education or specialization, you can fulfill your potential in your career and make it a success. But if your dream is to become a self-realized person, extraordinary efforts have to be made. If all your attention, time and effort go toward daily living, then what can you expect to know about spiritual life? There will come a time when you must decide what you want to do with the rest of your life, because whatever you acquire materially cannot be taken with you. What do we take with us?

All religions speak about life after death. What do you mean when you think of a soul entering heaven or the Oriental idea of rebirth? Unless you make changes now, in this life, how could you be any different after you die? What more would you know simply because you are free of the cage of your body? Try to imagine a vortex of energy—consciousness—that encapsulates all that you are mentally, emotionally and spiritually, and that includes the energy that controls the body, and memory itself. Science agrees that energy is indestructible. You can change energy, but you cannot totally destroy it or make it nonexistent. The vortex of energy could then assume another place to live, another time to express itself, cultivate itself, perfect itself. This is what could be reborn.

We can say, "But aren't philosophy and spiritual life a dream, too?" Yes, but they are a dream from which we can benefit, a dream that nourishes us differently, a dream that brings a greater state of awareness, and a dream that gives rise to quite a different mental power. When we clarify our ideals by asking, "What kind of person do I want to be?" that is also a dream, but it is within the realm of possibility. I can dream that it would be wonderful to be healthy, to have a positive attitude, and not only smile, but let that smile come from my heart. If the dream is entirely related to myself, then it is within my capacity to manifest it. But I have to recognize its importance and develop the powers to bring it about.

Some things we cannot bring about with the limited powers of mind we have today. I will not say they are impossible, but we do not have the necessary ability to keep the mind single-pointed over extended periods of time. We have to build up certain powers of the mind first, and then our dreams can become a reality. We have lost contact with the true knowledge of who we are. We have forgotten our Divine origin, our inheritance, and have become trapped in the encasement of human existence.

To help us understand our potential we can look at mythology, which is really the symbolic history of humanity. Consider the myth of the young gods from mid-heaven who descended to Earth, pulled by their own curiosity.[38] When they resided on the Earth for too long, enjoying themselves, their beautiful ethereal bodies began to harden. The ethereal body or vortex of energy, when too long exposed to the Earth's atmosphere, adjusted to it and finally lost its ability to return.

We are the young gods from mid-heaven. Or, if you take the story from the Bible, we are the fallen angels. If we take the very early Egyptian Gnostics' view, we are the soul descended into matter that enjoys the union so much that we do not want to return to our heavenly home. But God, who does not want to abandon the soul, makes sure that we eventually remember our origin, and long for our real home.

Think about it. How are you using your God-given intelligence? You can make the choice to become aware and to start the journey home.

If we direct our minds by focusing and concentrating on an image, we can discover the mind's powers. Leave the smorgasbord of images behind, choose a single one, and pursue it. See what happens. Choose an image that can change your life. That is precisely what you do with the Divine Light Invocation. You create in your mind an image of Divine Light, and fill your body with this Light. Light is a symbol for the Divine energy and has been used by many religions for many centuries. By practicing the Divine Light Invocation, you reinforce your desire to become a being of Light who will bring Light and joy into the lives of other people and greater joy and fulfillment into your own life. By continuously focusing on the Light and by inviting Light into your life, you will become a different person.

Here are the instructions for practicing the Divine Light Invocation, which is one of the most important practices for establishing and maintaining contact with the Light within.[39]With the Divine Light Invocation, you permeate all you are with Light. There is nothing greater than the Light, which is the most subtle symbol for the Divine. By permeating your whole body with Light, you automatically drive your ego out. Focus on this. You want to let the light of understanding, the light of love, grow. Your own growth and development will take place much more easily in the light of wisdom rather than in the artificial light of theoretical knowledge.

THE DIVINE LIGHT INVOCATION

Stand erect, feet shoulder-width apart. Keep the eyes closed and focus them on the space between the eyebrows. Inhale. Lift the arms above the head at the same time as you smoothly and gradually tense the whole body. The arms should be kept straight and the tension maintained throughout the body. Hold the tension and the breath. Make the following affirmation to yourself, with all the concentration possible:

I am created by Divine Light.
I am sustained by Divine Light.
I am protected by Divine Light.
I am surrounded by Divine Light.
I am ever growing into Divine Light.

Slowly lower the arms as you exhale and relax. Keep the eyes closed and use your imagination to *see* yourself standing in a shower of brilliant white Light. See the Light pouring down upon you, flowing into the body through the top of the head, filling your entire being. Now, without raising the arms, keeping them at your side, tense the body and inhale. Hold the tension and the breath. Mentally repeat the Invocation. Slowly exhale and relax.

During the second repetition, with the arms beside the body, concentrate on *feeling* a warm glow of Light suffuse your entire body, outside as well as inside. Acknowledge silently to yourself:

Every cell of this, my physical body, is filled with Divine Light. Every level of consciousness is illumined with Divine Light. The Divine Light penetrates every single cell of my being, every level of consciousness.
I have become a channel of pure Light. I am One with the Light.

The Divine Light Invocation is an exercise of will, as well as an act of surrender. Be receptive to the Light and accept that you are now a channel of Divine Light. Express your gratitude with deep feeling. Have the desire to share this gift with someone whom you wish to help. Turn your palms forward.

You can now share the Divine Light with any friend or relative. Keep the eyes closed and visualize him or her standing before you. Mentally open the doors of your heart center and let the Light stream forth toward the feet of this person. See the Light encircling the person and spiraling upward in a clockwise direction, enveloping the body completely. See the spiral moving high up into the sky, taking his or her image along with it. Finally the person merges into the source of the Light and becomes one with the Light. You may even lift your head to follow the spiral of Light, keeping the eyes closed. When the person has passed from your view, relax and silently give thanks for having the opportunity to help someone in need. Remember, in helping others we are also helping ourselves.

If your concentration weakens while you are practicing the Divine Light Invocation, repeat the exercises.

Learn to put people into a spiral of Light, and keep yourself in the Light so that only the Divine in you is actively in the foreground.

The Divine Light Invocation may be used as a mantra or positive affirmation, as well.[40] Repeat the words of the Invocation to yourself and see yourself surrounded by Divine Light in your daily life. It will help you to keep in touch with the Light within you and to see the Light in others around you.

EXERCISES AND REFLECTIONS

1. Use the Divine Light Invocation many times during the day. If you arehaving difficulty with another person, put that individual into the Light. It will diminish any hostility you may feel and any hostile individual will also slowly change (perhaps not to the satisfaction of your emotions, but everything will take place in due time). Do not let your practice become routine or it will no longer have an effect and will become a mechanical process that has no meaning. You have to involve the emotions, and you may find that the emotions are very helpful if they are used correctly.

2. Think about Divine Light. Reflect on each line of the mantra.

3. Try to contact the body of Light through your practice of the Divine LightInvocation. As long as you are alive, there is a tiny speck of energy—you can call it Light, you can call it life force—in every cell of your body. Recognizing your own energy and becoming aware of energy in every cell of your body is important. This concentrated focus takes time to develop. Start by cultivating the imagination, because creative imagination opens the door to a different kind of perception. Perceiving your own body as a mass of Light is an extraordinary experience that you will never, ever forget.

4. Another practice for gaining awareness of the Light is learning to see theLight around everything.[41] Take a grain of rice between two fingers and hold it up against the sky. Maintain your focus on the grain of rice until you see a halo of Light around it, a tiny force of Light emanating from it. When, over time, you have achieved the ability to see the grain of rice emanating Light, place the grain in a silver bowl and present the rice as an offering to the Divine. It can be part of the treasure chest of your efforts to move toward the Divine.

5. See if you can observe the shine of life in each petal of a freshly cutflower. Then watch it over the next few hours and the next few days. Can you see the shine from the petals slowly disappear, even though the color may not change? The energy, the inner Light, is gone. The same thing can happen with human beings—the body may die later, after the Light of the spirit is already gone.

6. When you feel miserable or depressed, you can turn the image of DivineLight into a more personal Divine image. It is just as if you are creating a balloon with your imagination and painting on it a picture of Jesus, Buddha, Divine Mother (whichever is your favorite), knowing that the energy that fills the balloon is Divine. The image satisfies the emotional need for personal contact with the Divine. The Light will be there when you are able to receive it, but the image will be there, created out of the Light, when you need the image. It is like seeing the Light in different frequencies, different pulses and different colors. One day the Light and the image may oscillate, so that you see first the image, then the Light, the image, the

Light. Light is the only image that is so fine, so ethereal, that any image you visualize can be dissolved into Light. Finally, images will dissolve into Light by themselves.

7. The whole process of working with dreams will bring about an evolutiontoward the Light, because the mind's production of the dream is nothing but a play of Light in different colors. Dreams give you the way to see yourself through their prism. If you put your activities into the Light, your dreams will also become quite different.

8. Even if you have an experience that is just a flight of fancy, you can stillwork with it and see if you can get to the bottom of it. Although it may be just your wishful thinking, your desires and imagination can prepare you for experiences of a more serious nature. If you want Light in your life, think about Light, invoke the Light with your imagination. That is the preparation. One day you will have it. You will know true experiences because they will turn your life around—you just cannot remain the same person.

9. The degree of your intensity in the practices relates to their effectiveness.You can support your direction by intensely concentrating, even for brief moments throughout the day, on a spiritual thought, a mantra, an image or a prayer, or by feeling an intense desire to be with the Divine.

chapter 22

DREAM? ILLUSION? REALITY?

You can expand your investigation of dreams in the waking state. Do not think of just one particular type of daydream, but ask yourself: "How is my whole life like a dream? Where do I make up my own nightmares and get involved in them?" Suddenly you may catch yourself and wake up, realizing that you are creating a mental reality that you do not need to stay involved in. Find out if there is another reality to which you can go—though not as an escape. You can never "escape" to a greater reality.

Sometimes you will see that this greater reality can be transmitted to you through a dream, and sometimes you will recognize that daily activity is like a good or a bad dream—that certain realities are not as solid as you think.

Think for a moment about how creative the mind is. We can produce an enormous amount through the power of the mind, if we really look at it. We can have an awareness that certain things exist only in our mind, nourished by our emotions. One example is psychosomatic illness, the product of imagination. Another is a woman who believes she is pregnant and has all the signs, even the placenta and the milk, but no baby. How did she produce these signs? She cannot tell you. But she had an almost fanatical desire to have a baby. All the power of her emotions went into that single-pointed idea in her mind, creating the process in her body. So the emotional power of desire can create a situation that is at least a partial fulfillment of the desire. Would you say the ability to create the changes in her body was real, or just an illusion, or a "partial" reality?

Some yogis do fantastic experiments and practices—for example, locking themselves for years in a single room without the influence of light, just to find out how creative the mind is. Yet at the same time, they take their dreams very seriously. Why would such people pay attention to dreams? Precisely because dreams can be the thorn that removes the thorn. By seeing how creative dreams are, they may come to contemplate reality and find out how each day is like another dream.

The experience of dreaming can be a model that helps us understand the unreality or illusions we create in our own lives. In dreams we suffer only temporarily, until we wake up. You may dream that you hurt yourself and experience the pain with great intensity. You may dream you are separated from someone you love and feel the emotional pain, until someone wakes you up. When you wake up to the greater reality of Cosmic Consciousness, you will see life and its suffering as a dream. But you have to experience this directly, not just entertain an intellectual concept about it.

Looking at life from the philosophical standpoint of *Maya* (that the world is illusion), you may ask, "If this waking life isn't real, why bother with the life of the unconscious?"

As long as you are walking around in a physical body that can feel aches and pains, you have to realize that this physical level of reality has some power. If a person has to have a leg amputated, you cannot say, "Your leg is just an illusion. You never had that leg in the first place." I know my body exists and has come into being by some means. If I say it is through the power of the mind, I have to reflect on what that means. If my leg were to be amputated, where is the power of mind that can create another leg? And if I have created the whole body, why can I not do this?

Mixing an intellectual understanding that "life is illusion" with the fact of our existence can create a great deal of confusion and uncertainty in daily life, making things very complicated. This confusion often happens when people read Eastern texts intellectually, without having really absorbed the teachings as they should be absorbed. We have to be careful and discriminating, and ask: "What is the reality of this physical life? What is the reality of the mind? What do I really know?" If you have only read about this idea without acquiring the knowledge from practices, you might imagine yourself among the elite of thinkers. But do you really know or have you just accepted and believed without thinking in depth?

"Knowing" means knowing from experience. To attain true knowledge you need extraordinary power. The mind requires the tremendous force of a rocket that can penetrate the gravitational field of the Earth and then is free in space. Once you go into the "outer space of the mind," you may indeed gain quite a different understanding. Only from that liberated perspective can you look at life and see it as illusion. While still living in the enclosed atmosphere of desires and the gross sensory perceptions, you cannot fool yourself and say, "I have heard about Liberation and I've read about it, so I know what it is." The mind is not capable of penetrating its barriers that easily.

What can you gain from brainstorming "reality" and "illusion" that you can apply in your daily life? At least discover where you create your own illusions. You have to be willing to face the untruths, the false beliefs and the tainted ideas that you have about yourself. Start with practical steps and take one step at a time. Lay a good foundation. Otherwise any Earth-shaking discovery can bring all your mental constructs crashing down. Once you know something from experience, you will never feel hurt if others disagree with your view. The foundation you have built becomes so strong that it cannot be shaken by any opposing concept.

From your exploration of daily life, you can then begin to investigate other levels of reality. What is the relationship between space, time and the unconscious? What are the different levels of consciousness? Right now if you were to try to contemplate seven levels of consciousness, you could not. You know to a limited extent—and not even accurately—three levels, because you live in the three-dimensional world. If you have some spiritual experiences, you have put your foot slightly into a new dimension, the fourth dimension. But even if you have had a great number of spiritual experiences, you still cannot anticipate what the fifth dimension would be like, or the sixth, or beyond. You have to lay the foundation before you can explore even the possibility of a fourth, fifth or sixth dimension.

At one point you may question your understanding of time. From a certain perspective you might understand that reincarnation has meaning only as long as you accept time as you now know it. When you go beyond the general understanding of time and space, even reincarnation disappears. The one hundred thousand lifetimes that you may have had to this point are simply perceived as one life; what you consider your current life is like a day between nights. Just as you do not cut your life into little bits and pieces and think you are a different person at each stage of life, so all lifetimes in a sequence of one hundred thousand may really only be one.

So ask yourself, “What is reality?” A word for “reality” exists in all languages. If the word exists, there must be something that *is* real. The human mind cannot think of anything that is nonexistent. We are usually aware of the physical, tangible world, the world that we experience through the body, and that includes the universe with all its galaxies. That is one reality. But what about the reality of the energy that pervades it all?

In yogic thinking we live in three worlds—the physical world, the mental world and the spiritual world. That means we can also have illusions on the physical level, on the mental level and on the spiritual level. We have to be sure that our spiritual experiences are true experiences, not imaginary movies. But although we can have illusions about the Higher Self and the spiritual world, that does not mean that the spiritual reality itself is an illusion. The physicist may not be able to see the particles, but the traces are recognizable. If the traces are there, then something must exist that created the traces.

How can we recognize the traces of the cosmic reality? Every day you breathe. Can you separate your breath from the air around you? Your breath becomes visible only under certain conditions, in certain temperatures. Those outward conditions are not the result of your own power. In the same way, every now and then Cosmic Energy will let you know of its presence by creating a condition where you can see that power within yourself.

Here is another example. You might stand overlooking the lake and say, "How beautiful this lake is!" But what do you mean by "lake"? Lake is water, and water is a combination of two gases. Yet you do not see two gases constantly intermingling. In the same way, a certain reality is not necessarily so tangible to your senses that you can see it in its original state. We have to overcome the limitations of our senses on the gross level.

As you sit, you know your body, you know your size, you know your weight, you know your reflection in the mirror. But that which came into existence and made the decision to manifest, what does that look like? You cannot even know what your own self-created thoughts look like unless you give them an image. An invention may start from very abstract calculations, but if it is to manifest, there has to be a picture in someone's mind, nourished by the desire to create and by the power of imagination.

How does the power of imagination connect illusion and reality? Where does illusion end and reality begin?

The dream of flying probably arose from a desire for freedom, a desire to move without restraint. The image of flying preceded the creation of the machine that could manifest the desire. If you had dreamed about an airplane before airplanes existed, that dream would have been your illusion. But if you took your dream and invented an airplane, that manifestation would have a tangible reality. Once whatever you dream about comes into manifestation, it has a certain reality. Once the airplane existed, further ideas arose rapidly, developing the thing itself, making it more and more complex, faster, bigger, until years later we developed jets, and now we have rockets that can take us to the moon and beyond. Once we have created something, events take their own course. But everything that is now manifest started at some time as an intangible idea.

So the relationship between illusion and reality has to be very carefully contemplated. If we had not had a desire to fly, the airplane would never have been created. The moment you pick up an idea by the sensitivity to the creative power, this idea takes hold of you and, in turn, breeds a desire to manifest. Then you get busy scheming how you can manifest your desire. And if your desire is single-pointed, you will get it. It will manifest—in due time and in proportion to the degree of your intensity. Then when it is created and it exists, you cannot say that it is an illusion. The illusory force, having been very subtle at first, has now condensed. The idea has condensed into the manifestation of whatever we desire.

Let us assume that we once existed without this body, that consciousness existed as energy. You were consciousness per se, and had all the perceptions associated with your senses. But now we come to an impasse because it is impossible to imagine energy-as-such. Even nuclear physicists, who have exceptionally well-trained minds for abstract thinking, cannot think of something intangible, unimaginable. So we have to create an image for that pure energy in order to be able to deal with it. Then you have to remind yourself that you have done so, in order not to confuse the symbol with the energy itself, which cannot be explained by words.

We can imagine consciousness as a vortex of energy like a tornado. Although we cannot see the air current itself, we can see its funnel shape from the dust that the tornado has picked up. Similarly, consciousness holds the dust and seeds of memory and past actions. And now we can come to another understanding of human existence here on Earth. Life has always existed here, but perhaps the human mind needed a properly prepared vehicle for receiving the energy of consciousness. The brain is that vehicle, and the body is the vehicle for the brain. Once the body has manifested, we cannot deny its reality.

At some point we have to recognize that our body is not what we usually think it is, but is a vehicle to be used for the attainment of pure consciousness. The body, in other words, has to be recognized as a spiritual tool with which to attain the ultimate. Then we do not deny the physical reality, but recognize a greater one.

As you expand your thinking, you will see that your mental reality is transformed. This transformation is a process—new concepts are born and others will "reincarnate" within ourselves. Eventually we will move toward the state of liberation from all limitations that are a weight, that are restrictive, and that keep us in our self-fabricated prisons.

What is dreaming up this life? Get in touch with that and you will be in touch with the reality of your innermost self.

There is a saying in the Puranas[42] that Vishnu dreams the world into existence. Life is the Divine Play, although sometimes the dream looks random.

We can see that each of us creates our own world by dreaming different types of dreams. As we become more aware, we can start to ask, "Why should I dream about problems and difficulties when I am the creator of my dream and have the power to change it?"

We can even dream about all the beauties of spiritual life, but we might find that our own materials—the threads from which we weave the dream— are not always strong, or clean, or long enough. We might make mistakes in knotting, or tie some threads too tightly. So our dream cannot be as perfectly realized as it is in our minds or desires.

We have to learn how to weave the thread of our dreams into the design of the Divine Play and not get tangled in the attachments of the world.

EXERCISES AND REFLECTIONS

1. Learn to watch all the images flashing by in the mind without identifyingwith any of them, because if you identify with them you become involved with them. You do not want to become unnecessarily involved with the contents of the mind. Write down those thoughts and images that come again and again, and finally look at them squarely, straight on: Is it so important? Is it my ego? Do I need to assert myself? What happens if I don't? Am I stepped on? Or am I just experiencing karma coming back to me?

2. It is best to practice reflection before attempting to practice meditation.When you can recognize what is going on and throw out the creations of your mind, and finally put a stop to them, then you are beginning to make progress. The problem in the West is that most people have not done the preparations before they try to meditate. If you do not try to sit motionlessly for three to five hours and face the wrestling of your mind, you just do not know what the mind can do.

3. Put certain pictures and objects in your room—a picture of the Buddha,Jesus, Divine Mother, Krishna—whatever image of the Divine most appeals to you. Whenever your eyes glance at them, immediately, by the law of thought association, you are reminded that you have been

dreaming, daydreaming, that you have clouded the awareness of your true nature, of your true state of awareness, of your Higher Self.

4. Often in the West we assume that reality is something concrete. If youthink, for example, that the table is solid, I suggest that you sit and stare at it for ten minutes and then record what you see. Even science tells us that what *appears* to be, may not be what is. Can you look at a large lake and see it as a combination of two gases?

5. Observe yourself. That which you look at, do you see it? What is the act ofseeing? And what is it that you see? Is there indeed a moment where the three —the seer, the act of seeing and what is seen—blend into one?

6. Ask yourself:

- What are my concepts of dream, illusion and reality?
- Is there more than one level of reality?
- Where does illusion end and reality begin?
- What is the reality of a dream experience?
- What is the reality of daily life experience?
- If I knew that everything was illusion, would that remove the dramatic, painful obstacles in daily life?

PART THREE

DREAM YOGA

chapter 23

DREAM YOGA PRACTICES

Dream Yoga requires first the willingness to train the mind even to remember dreams, and then the discipline to carry through specific practices. You have to become aware of the personal language of your own unconscious, which is based on the impressions from many lifetimes and on the influences of your present life. You also have to deal with what emerges from the unconscious in your daily life, and discover how you create your own illusions and realities. After you have established a good foundation by understanding your own symbolism, and after you have explored mind, illusion and reality as presented in the earlier parts of this book, you may be ready for more specific Dream Yoga practices.

Some of these practices may seem a bit disconcerting because you have to break with well-established habits, not only of thinking but even of living and sleeping, if Dream Yoga is to be truly successful. For example, you may think you need eight hours of sleep every night, but that is not necessarily so. Because in the same way that you nourish your body by what you eat, you nourish your mind and heart by what you think and do. Spiritual practices nourish the feelings of the heart and release the pressure of emotions.[43] By nourishing the heart, a higher part of the mind will eventually open. Then, if you really want the Divine, you will experience quite an extensive influence of the Divine through your dreams.

The most important quality in the practice of Dream Yoga is your sincerity. Insights will arise from the sincerity of your hope, willingness and receptivity. Your constant focus on the Divine will bring you closer—both when you are awake and when you are asleep. Whatever you do in your waking life—driving your car, washing dishes or typing on the computer—you have to cultivate the awareness that you are always in the presence of the Divine. If I want to know who you are, I have to become involved with you. I have to be able to observe your responses to me. If I do not get any response,

I will try harder until I do. It is the same in becoming involved with the Divine. I have to try until I get a response. When I elicit even a faint response, I have something to build hope on. If I stay involved, which means to be in the service of the Most High, it is likely that I will receive a stronger response.

Staying involved with the Divine means developing the ability to visualize at will—a feeling, a thought, a Divine image, Light. This requires concentration, the ability to maintain single-pointed focus. To practice Dream Yoga, you need to control the mind, which is extremely difficult and requires the same intensity of concentration that a surgeon needs in performing a new type of surgery. You have to be right there—not somewhere else at the same time. When I was first learning to develop single-pointedness, I would sit with a big box of matches in my lap, and attempt to say the first line of a four-line mantra, keeping out any other intruding thoughts. Any time a thought came in, I would drop a match onto the floor. When the match box was empty, I realized how difficult it is for the mind to stay with one single line of thought. I often suggest that people work with their favorite prayer in the same way. When you do achieve that concentrated focus, you come to a resting place where the body-mind no longer interferes. The body-mind is simply pushed aside, and you may have an extraordinary dream or experience.

Eventually, through daily practice of reflection leading to meditation, the power you gain will carry you through day and night, sleep and dream. When you have imbued your mind intensely with a desire for the Most High, this desire itself will become a guiding light. As you learn to keep your focus directed, you increase the chance of contacting or recognizing the Light in sleep.

Working with Dream Yoga will bring you to the point where you can discover that the spiritual world is not an illusion. The mind is capable of such incredible dreams that you will be challenged to ask, "What is real? And how do I move from this world to that?" You become aware that everything is relative. Is your dream the reality?

Instructions for Dream Yoga are part of Eastern yoga practices,[44] but these are not easily understood by a modern Westerner since the teachings were part of a different culture. Certain cultural laws become anchored in the human mind. Those laws become a forceful, controlling reality in our lives. Only under a great threat (or more rarely, a great passion) will we be persuaded to go beyond them.

Often, too, terminology is used in the Eastern texts that is not explained because it was written for students immersed in the philosophy. Another cause for misunderstanding is that the Eastern mind functions differently from the Western—the Westerner takes everything literally, whereas the Eastern teacher expects you to understand through intuitive perception. For example, one of the Dream Yoga instructions is to investigate carefully what causes rapid awakening from dreams; if there is too much tension, you should relax more. You are not told *how* to relax, but obviously what is meant is not just lying down and relaxing your muscles. You relax by looking at that which makes you tense.

However, I think that the essential meaning, technique and aim of Dream Yoga teachings are quite understandable to us and can be put into practice now, to our great benefit. When I recognized that what I loosely termed my "sleep" was really a different state of mind, and "dream" was often a meditative experience, I asked myself how I could help other people attain this same state. The following practices are ones that I have used and can recommend to anyone wishing to get in touch with that greater reality.

First train yourself to observe the mind and to retain the memory of your thoughts while falling asleep. Watch the images that flit by and explode into emotions. Observe your breath. Breath is the best indicator of balanced or unbalanced emotions—emotions that can be as harsh as anger and violence, or as sweet as attachment and other illusions. Observe the many colors of emotions, as well as the shades from black to white. Try to *watch* yourself fall asleep.

Practice holding your rosary or your mala, or a special ring or stone, throughout the night. Use any object with meaning from your tradition and culture. You might choose a sacred object or a stone from your favorite pebble beach. Or you can write a prayer or a very important intuitive thought on a small strip of paper and roll this paper into a tiny roll. Then try to keep the object in your hand without letting it go; if you do let it go, train yourself to wake up immediately. This indicates that your awareness is focused where you intended it to be.

Then you can begin the practice of visualization. Create an image in your mind of the Divine Source. For most people it will be easier to concentrate on a concrete form than an abstract idea, just as it is easier to visualize a beautiful flower and to imagine its fragrance than it is to think of the flower as a combination of chemicals. Light is the most subtle image grasped by the mind. The same spiral of white Light that you visualize going up in the Divine Light Invocation, you should now see surrounding your body or your entire bed like a cocoon as you sleep. Then throughout the night try to maintain that connection with the Light—"holding the Light" as you sleep.

Holding the Light during sleep is one of the key instructions for Dream Yoga. How can you do this? By becoming very familiar with the Divine Light Invocation and by exercising your ability to visualize the Light. Being able to maintain contact with the Light during sleep requires rigorous practice on a daily basis. Eventually, through this regular practice, the power will become more steady.

Bring in the mantra as your last thought in the period immediately before falling asleep. Your mantra might be the Divine Light Mantra, or hari om, or om namah sivaya, or the Divine Mother Prayer.[45] If you need help in removing your mental-emotional obstacles, call on Siva. If you feel you have lost your way, call on Krishna to play the flute and call you home. You can also use any sacred words that symbolize the Most High to you—calling on the name of the Virgin Mother or Jesus, or repeating "Jesus loves me" from the Christian tradition, or repeating a line from a prayer in whatever religious tradition you come from. See if you can maintain this involvement with your mantra or your prayer throughout the night.

When I first started watching dreams, I made a pact: "I will remember my dreams only when there is something important for me to know and to learn, but otherwise I will stay with the mantra." When, through constant practice, you can keep the mantra going until you reach the point where you wake up in the morning with the mantra, then you are over a big hurdle, because during the six or more hours that you sleep, the most important part of your mind is with the mantra. Then you do not need to worry if you have time for meditation in the day because you have accumulated the mantric power in yourself so intensely that you do not even lose it in sleep. But this is only one plateau. Do not rest there, although you can at least be assured that all the sacrifices you have made to reach this point were worth it.

The gradual development of the ability to remain focused on the Divine word and image depends on how much work you do on yourself. It is almost a superhuman effort if you have not first removed the psychological obstacles. All practices have to be done with awareness. If you find that you are going off into a trance, minimize your practice. All powers that come to us, even Divine powers, should be under control. No power that we cannot control is good for us, even if it comes directly from the Divine. But in conjunction with the practice of awareness, there will be no trance.

Some practitioners of Dream Yoga sleep in a certain position to try to remain aware while the body sleeps. The sleep position recommended for Dream Yoga is to lie on your left side (with one leg drawn up to relax the abdomen), close your right nostril with the back of your left hand, and breathe throughout the night through your left nostril in order to have only the spiritual current active for regenerating the physical body and the various levels of mind. This position also influences the contents of your dreams.

See what happens and find out what kind of dream you have in the morning. It is quite possible you will turn over ten minutes after falling asleep. But you can gradually train yourself to sleep at least a few hours on your left side, breathing only through your left nostril. Eventually you may be able to hold the position for four or five hours. Be truly observant and make careful notes.

This alone—maintaining a certain alertness and letting just the body sleep—is a very difficult achievement and will take quite some time. However, if you have ever been deprived of sleep, for instance as many people are during wars, you may have learned that this is possible. I remember being on the subway in Europe during the Second World War, and while my body was standing asleep, something in my mind would be aware and say, "Six stations from now you must get out." I knew precisely where I was, what I was doing and where I was going. These peculiar states of mind appear extraordinary only because we have not paid enough attention or tried to find out how the mind works.

I remember when my Guru was going to explain the position to me, he said, "First show me how you sleep." We were out on the open patio, which had a cement floor, but that didn't matter. I lay down on the cement to show him. "Aah! And why do you sleep this way?"

"I always sleep this way. I don't know why." My natural sleep position was, in fact, the exact position prescribed for Dream Yoga. Past lives? This is possible, but it is also possible to pick up what is needed from other minds, because the interaction of minds becomes quite expansive. The busier we are, the less it happens, of course.

One of the Eastern Dream Yoga practices is to focus on the throat center and to worship the guru in the throat center.[46] The guru in the throat chakra is something that can only be understood if you have worked with the Kundalini system. Then you will know that the throat center is the center of surrender. To follow instructions, you have to surrender. To listen to someone, especially the guru within, you have to surrender the merry-goround of mental conversation in your own head; otherwise, you will not hear what is said. The word "guru" does not always refer to a physical human being. The guru, in this case, is the essence, the energy, and the capacity to surrender. That which is surrendered—self-will—has used energy to express itself, frequently as stubbornness, throughout life. When the expression of self-will is removed and surrender is achieved, then by the sincerity of your undertaking that energy becomes a guiding guru in future actions.

Some schools of thought encourage people to manipulate the contents of their dreams in order to create a situation that they want. But do you not already know what you want? Why would you need to manipulate your dreams? To what end? If you already have illusions about yourself and do not even realize it, and then you try to manipulate your dreams, you will never know who you really are. All the personality aspects will just fight among themselves. Many people are able to manipulate dreams that are at a psychological level. But if you want to step out of the psychological and have contact with the Divine, you have to maintain your focus on the Divine and *surrender* to the wisdom within. Then your dreams will change in a way that is quite dramatic.

When you can maintain the Light in sleep, wrapping yourself in Light and filling yourself with Light, you will stay in a receptive frame of mind, open to Divine influences. When the self-generating power of the Divine Light Mantra is achieved and can be extended into sleep, if dreams do come they often take on a very different character. They become direct messages. You can contact your Divine essence and learn that there are as yet undiscovered places of Light from which great wisdom emanates.

Your continuous work with Dream Yoga will make it possible for you to approach a certain part of the mind more intensely. When you have passed through certain "gates," as I call them—the first being the psychological, then the instructive—you will eventually come in contact with a hidden place of the mind, a higher mind that most people rarely even know they have. What you discover is not something given by an external power. You have just cleared the garbage away and let emerge what has always been there.

Then you will have very different dreams—dreams that seem more real than life itself, dreams that will in fact give a perspective of more than one life. Through this kind of dream, you open a secret door—a door to the Eternal Light. Then you begin to realize that you are not who you think you are. You may have climbed Jacob's Ladder far enough to say, "There are no further rungs to climb. I can now be lifted up by the power of the Light."

But an exclusive focus on the Light is necessary if you want dreams to lead you to the Light, and to a recognition of the Light within. If you are only theoretical, you will never achieve anything. To experience the hidden meaning of dreams, you need to have an intense commitment to the pursuit of awareness. As long as there is greed—not necessarily for material gain but for recognition, to be seen and heard—certain types of dreams will not occur because the degree of surrender, absolute receptivity and the strength of intuition are lost.

While we now live in the physical body, which is a "dream body" that cannot go with us at death, we will eventually live in a body of Light. This has to occur. Sleeping focused on the Light is a preparation for death, which will make it possible to be reborn into a higher state of understanding and eventually into the enlightened state.

SUMMARY OF DREAM YOGA PRACTICES

- Practice concentration exercises to gain single-pointedness of mind
- Watch your breath, thoughts and emotions before sleep.
- Hold an object—a mala or stone or written prayer— throughout the night.
- Visualize yourself surrounded in a cocoon of Light as you go to sleep.
- Keep the mantra as your last thought before falling asleep.
- Sleep on your left side, closing your right nostril and breathing through the night through your left nostril.
- Practice surrender and listening to the voice of the inner guru.

EXERCISES AND REFLECTIONS

1. Find out how many repetitions it takes until you can say aloud a prayer ormantra without any other intruding thought. One way to practice this is to close your eyes and recite the prayer, line by line. As soon as you have an intruding thought, open your eyes and begin again. It is very important to not try to cheat yourself. Instead, just accept where you are at the moment and recognize that you have more work to do to increase concentration.

2. Daily diary writing and reflection become increasingly important. Askyourself:

- What is dream?
- What is fantasy?
- What are emotional needs?
- What is my heart reflecting?
- What do I reflect to other people?
- Can I be a seed of inspiration to others?
- Can I receive seeds of inspiration?

3. Dream Yoga is done in conjunction with sharpening sense perceptions forgreater awareness—to hear with the inner ear, to smell, taste, see, touch the Divine presence. Because dreams are very strongly influenced by your senses, it is very important to know precisely how your five senses function. The power of the senses needs to be carefully investigated.

Is that wonderful being you have seen in the eyes of the inner mind a fantasy? Wishful thinking? Or is it really a kind of Divine presence?

If you smell roses and violets or sandalwood, what does it indicate? What insights arise?

When you have a dream in which you have been seeing, can you recall that dream again from the sense of hearing?

Recall the dream, each time from a different sense.

4. Observe the effects on your dreams as you practice the Dream Yogaexercises. It is necessary to go slowly, to assess your situation again and again, and to take careful note of your thoughts and feelings, and even of the physical aspect of sleeping in the prescribed position. Emotional reactions and moods need to be dealt with and carefully noted down to make the picture complete.

chapter 24

CONFIRMING DREAMS

As you learn to concentrate on the Light and mantra, and as you develop an attitude of surrender and total reliance on your dreams, you will find that dreams give you exactly what you need. It may take some time before you receive insights at the highest levels because if you have neglected your inner being, it takes time to re-establish contact. Be patient and remember that it takes nine months even to be born.

Eventually you will have wonderful dreams—dreams of Divine guidance—confirmations, instructions and inspirations. You might have an intense period where your dreams are very inspirational, but then at another time find that all inspiration suddenly vanishes for some years. In the interim, before the elevated dreams return, you will probably receive dreams of purification—"rinsing the mud off the Cadillac," as I sometimes call the process.

The more you truly want the Divine contact and guidance and the more you can say thank you for even the smallest awareness or insights that arise, the more cooperation you will receive from your Higher Self. If you wait for some extraordinary vision of Lord Krishna, you can miss the sparkling little insights that have their own greatness. Even a small light can help us find our way; we do not always need a magnificent sunrise. Whenever you have an insight, take time to reflect on it. To help interpret your dreams you can practice what I call a "prayer without words" by sitting quietly in a receptive mood with your hands upturned in your lap. The position is your silent affirmation that "Whatever I am given, I want to understand."

Take every insight as a milestone on the Path of the Light. If there are long gaps between milestones, keep going nevertheless. Sometimes you can ask your dreams for a confirmation: "Please let me know if I am still going in the right direction." The confirmation will come.

I learned that I could depend on my dreams to tell me when I was doing the right thing and when I was not. Therefore I could take refuge in my dreams. I could completely rely on the inner guru to respond to my needs.

What were my needs? I had no experience in running an ashram. I had spent only six months at Sivananda Ashram in India, and during that time I was concentrated on my spiritual development. I certainly did not receive instructions in administration, and what I did learn came from observing those in charge—listening to the intonation of their voices and watching the expression on their faces, because I did not speak the language.

So when I had established the ashram in Canada, as my Guru had requested, I was often very worried: "Am I making wise decisions? Am I handling problems correctly?" I wished that I could receive some indication that I was on the right track. I remember rushing to the front door whenever mail was delivered, unconsciously hoping for a letter that would answer all my questions—which, of course, could never come. My lack of experience was so great that my only hope was to surrender and to try to maintain contact with the Divine. I learned to rely totally on my dreams—and they proved to be very reliable indeed.

Prior to the following dream, which I had during the formative years of the ashram, one of the young residents had challenged me by saying that there were so many religious fanatics thinking they were doing the will of God, how did I know *I* was? Of course this was the very question I was agonizing over. I was still at the stage where I had many doubts about myself: "Am I really good enough? I know I don't have a pure mind—why should I have been chosen for the Divine Work?" Then I had this dream.

Repairing the Road

I had to walk down a certain road. When I saw that it was very rough and difficult to walk upon, I decided to bring a tool with me. The tool looked something like a wooden snow shovel, and I used it to push the snow, mud, stones and dirt to the right and left sides, out of the way. When I found some ice underneath, I turned the tool upside down since it had a steel point at the other end, and I broke the ice quite easily with it. As I worked, the road became clear and clean and easy to walk upon.

Suddenly I came upon a big hole right in the middle of the road. I stopped and filled it in, then tramped and stamped down the earth to make sure it was level with the rest. Now the road was smooth and anyone could go back and forth easily at any time.

I could have jumped over the hole, I thought, but then what would happen to others who might come along, especially in the dark?

The next morning the same young man who had challenged me asked if

I had had a dream. He was usually very critical, but when I told him this dream I saw his eyes suddenly fill with tears. In a quiet voice he said he would not question again why I, a woman, had been chosen for the work. So the dream and the interaction that followed confirmed to me that I was doing the work appropriately. To me the road symbolized spiritual life, and the tool represented the spiritual tools I had been given. This particular tool was not a refined one—not something that required the precise skill of a jeweler—but it was the right tool for this job. With it I could clear the path of obstacles, making it easier for others to walk upon, and I could fill in the gaps that might otherwise be dangerous for those who would follow.

As we try to maintain contact with the Divine even in our sleep, our spiritual concepts take on a very definite form. In the following dream, I am again given a confirmation even as I express uncertainty about my ability.

Krishna's Flute

A messenger brought me a beautiful parcel wrapped in paper with little roses on it, and a pink ribbon. There was a card: "To Radha, my beloved."

The messenger said, "I am bringing this gift from Lord Krishna. Do you know who he is?"

"Yes, I know." I was overjoyed. Then I opened the parcel. It was a flute. "But I can't play the flute," I said.

Then the messenger asked, "Would you be given a flute if you couldn't play it?"

As human beings we are often beset with feelings of inferiority, or even sinfulness and inadequacy. My own Guru realized that not only women of the Orient, but women all over the world have had little chance to develop selfconfidence and determination. That is why when Swami Sivananda initiated me, he said, "Put my name (Sivananda) in front of yours (Radha)." He knew this would give a boost to my self-esteem. When I told Swami Sivananda that I was not perfect enough or holy enough to establish an ashram in the West, he smiled and said, "Just be Lord Krishna's flute. Let the Divine play the melody. Learn to listen, and all will be well." And now the flute had arrived!

Krishna's flute is a marvelous symbol. A bamboo flute is really just a stick with holes in it that cannot hold anything at all. If you pour water into it, the water will run out. And a flute cannot produce any music by itself. Krishna's flute can be heard only when the Divine gives the intuitive perception of its will, and we can surrender to it. Over the years I began to understand that while quick intellectual answers might pop into my mind, it was better to put them aside and wait for the voice of spiritual intuition to be heard.

Some time later, I had the same dream again but:

This time I took out the flute, played it immediately, and said, "The others will wonder at how well I can play."

The "others" were the people who gave me the sharpest criticism.

After having this dream of Krishna's flute, I understood that I needed to become an instrument through which the Divine could pour its melody. That meant not only listening intuitively, but being willing to say what was needed, even if the other person did not like it. If I was concerned about whether people liked me or not, I could not do the work, I could not play the flute. This was my experience and it is something that I can recall in an instant and remind myself: "Never mind—it doesn't matter if anybody likes me. Just be Lord Krishna's flute."

The other saying that my Guru often used was "the milk of Divine Wisdom." He told me to be a spiritual mother to all, and that the mother has the milk before the baby is born. Somehow this symbolism penetrated my mind and became quite real in the following dream.

Feeding the Babies

A woman wearing many long skirts said to me, "There are many babies and they are very hungry. You should nourish them."

I said, "But I'm not a mother."

"Oh, don't make such a fuss," she said, and opened my blouse. She put one baby on each breast, saying, "You have two breasts. Put one here, the other there, and this bigger child can stand here and wait." He looked about two years old.

I was amazed that I would have milk to give. I looked over my shoulder, thinking the milk must come from somewhere else because I couldn't believe I would have any.

Then this same large woman came and took the first babies away. I saw the little two-year-old standing there, waiting, and behind him I suddenly saw that there was a whole army of people lined up, waiting—babies, children and adults. I started to get up, thinking that I would be here forever, when two heavy hands pushed me back to my seat, and the enormous woman who was now standing behind me said, "You will sit here as long as I need you!" Some people came with little buckets, and one person even had a frying pan.

The dream reassured me that I could do what my Guru had asked of me. Somehow—even though I could not understand how it was possible—the milk of Divine Wisdom was given. When I look back now, I see that there was, indeed, an army of people, spiritual babies of all sizes and shapes, passing through the ashram wanting to be nourished. But it was quite a strange experience having to sit there with this enormous being standing behind me and holding me down with her hands on my shoulders. It had an impact that I can hardly describe. There is no question of choice when Divine Mother wants us on the job.

Dreams like these gave me the strength to face the most formidable obstacles and the greatest challenges. Once I had the clear confirmation from the inner guru that I was going in the right direction, it did not matter if people disagreed with my approach or found fault with my personality. I tried to please the Divine, not other people.

So dreams can give us a deep inner knowing that helps us to develop the strength we need to pursue the goal. When we place our trust in the Divine, we will certainly experience the influence of the Divine through our dreams.

EXERCISES AND REFLECTIONS

1. After writing down your dream, sit for a few moments in a receptiveposition, palms upturned in your lap. Silently repeat the affirmation, "I want to understand whatever I have been given." Allow the interpretation of your dream to arise from within.

2. Review your dreams from the week and collect your insights, like preciousgems. What light do they shed on your life and direction at this time? Put your insights into action and find out what the results are.

3. Ask your dreams, "Am I doing the right thing?" Then, wait for the answer.

Through your own experience you will gain trust in the inner guru.

4. Ask yourself:
    - What are my needs at this time?
    - How do I distinguish between needs and desires?
    - How are my dreams responding to my real needs?

5. Find out if you have had dreams where your spiritual concepts take form. What is the message?

chapter 25

INSTRUCTIVE DREAMS

The area of the spirit is capable of transmitting quite a different kind of guidance to the human being in us through our intuition. As you work with your dreams you will discover that there is not just emotional meaning in dreams; there is also knowledge from other levels. That knowledge is available to us at all times, but we have to acquire a certain skill and we have to prepare to receive it. If I have a 15-watt bulb, I can expect only a dim light.

If I want more light, I have to provide the lamp with a more powerful bulb—40-watt, 60-watt, 100-watt, 200-watt. But there is also a limitation to the lamp, which is only wired for so much. In the same way, we may be capable of handling only a limited amount of spiritual energy. Through a number of experiences, we have to become prepared to receive Divine knowledge and to recognize its source.

When you take a prayerful attitude with a deep desire to know what you should do, you can receive explicit directions in no uncertain terms. I had several dreams in which I was given very direct instructions. The following dream shows just how straightforward and useful that advice can be—both for our own development and for helping others. A voice spoke directly to me, as follows.

Instructions

"You should first cut away the roots from the trees around you that have become intertwined with your own. They represent others' concepts that you have allowed to slip in. Watch for wrong acceptance of authority.

"You were shown in previous dreams that you have great wealth. What makes you think you should just keep it in your purse? Stop being afraid that you will create karma. Take a onedollar bill at a time, break it into change and start with the coins. But do something with it. What is not put to use is taken away.

"Do not worry about making mistakes. Remember, Divine Grace is always available to those who do the Divine Work. Keep watching your dreams—they will show you when something is wrong, truly wrong. But you will sail in big storms without a drop of water spilling into your boat, so there is no need to worry.

"Talk to people mentally if you cannot reach them otherwise. You can start by sitting quietly by yourself and talking in your own mind to that ill woman you are concerned about, at the same time wrapping her in Light. This will help remove the garbage from her unconscious. Every little clearing will bring her great relief. Do this with everyone you wish to help. In this way you will first light a candle in their unconscious. In time, as they get used to the Light, you can increase its strength.

"You must understand that many tools are needed simultaneously—a coarse broom for the coarse dirt, a fine broom for the dust. You must get all your tools in proper working order, which means developing your powers of mind. When you are given a new tool, add it to what you have been given. Otherwise you are like a child who, when given one toy, forgets about all the others.

"Work is expected from you now and a good output."

So when we ask to have our dream messages straight, we will get them straight. Who was the sender of the message? I have considered different possibilities. I could say the inner guru or the Higher Self. If consciousness can survive after a physical being has disappeared, I could speculate that it was the consciousness of another that was influencing me through the dream. Perhaps the message was a reflection of my own past knowledge being transmitted. There was no doubt that the words were wise.

Cutting away roots meant taking responsibility for my own ideas and clearing out those concepts that had become entangled with mine through conditioning. So I started uprooting ideas that were based on culture, education, social status, tradition. I struggled to free myself from the values of the family—traditional ideas about what was good and bad, which were based only on social rules and had nothing to do with the spiritual path. I discovered in which areas I was imitating my mother, my grandmother and my teachers. Many of their ideas were not really my convictions, so why should I continue to carry them? As I worked with freeing my roots, I had a sense of breathing more easily.

When I began to observe those people whom I had considered very holy and knowledgeable, I started to see that some of them could talk wonderfully about spiritual ideas, but they did not put their words into practice in their lives. It took me quite some time to recognize how I had accepted false authority, probably because I had been looking for encouragement and wanted others to do what I could not yet do.

The fear of making mistakes and creating karma had sometimes crippled my ability to take action. In the early years of my spiritual life I felt I did not have enough discrimination to act wisely. But I had to *learn* to make decisions, which is why my Guru did not respond to the specific questions in my letters. This fear of creating karma followed me around for a long time because I had become so aware of my thoughts. I was overly anxious about every wrong thought, every wrong action, and worrying about how I could have let them happen. "Do not worry about making mistakes" was an important lesson for me to learn. Now from my own experience, I give people in new positions the same advice: "Don't worry if you make mistakes —it is bound to happen. We learn by trial and error."

This dream gave me invaluable instructions about the best way to help certain people. When I practiced the suggested method I found that when my intensity was strong enough, the prayers, mental conversation and Light would have results. The prayers and Light could take people out of their regular patterns and lift them to quite a different, much higher level. But if the person who was meant to receive the Light had even stronger resistance, then there was nothing more I could do.

"Keep watching your dreams—they will show you when something is wrong, truly wrong."

Here was a dream telling me that I could depend on my dreams. When we can listen, when we can free ourselves of the prisons created by a sense of personal inadequacy, fear of criticism and rejection, then we begin to clear the way for the messages from a greater reality to come through.

And we can ask, "What are the realities of the dreaming mind?"

EXERCISES AND REFLECTIONS

1. Review your dreams to discover instructive dreams. You cannot receivethis kind of dream until you learn to listen. If you cannot listen in waking life, how can you hear the voice of the inner guru in dreams? Practice listening in daily life.[47]

2. Are you sincerely seeking directions? Would you follow the instructionsgiven to you by your inner guru?

When I was asking myself, "How would I know the will of God? How would I know whether or not I could surrender to that will?" I realized that it was imperative to have some way of knowing, since my Guru was so far away that he could not provide direct guidance. I decided I would do a surrender practice. I chose a very critical person from my environment, put that person into the Light for a week, and at the end of the week followed every suggestion, order or demand the individual made during the next week. I gradually extended the surrender practice to two weeks, three weeks, and finally three months. I made it clear to myself before I started that I would not do anything that would go against my conscience, but I would not let any financial expenses stand in the way of surrender.

If you decide to try this practice, notice your responses and reactions. They will show you where self-will is active. This process exercises your ability to surrender to the Divine.

3. To have direct dreams you have to overcome pride and be willing to admityour mistakes. Pray for the courage to look at things straight on and the strength to deal with what comes up. If you are earnest in your request, direct dreams will come. They can save you a great deal of time.

4. Make a conscious effort in your waking state to set your conscious mindaside and listen to the voice of intuition. If you want to discover and develop this reflective mode in yourself, observe the transition time of dusk or dawn. Then ask yourself:What is the dawn or the dusk of my mind? What keeps me from being in that twilight space?

chapter 26

DREAM EXPERIENCES

When you are already working with your psychological problems and you are sincerely willing to learn, then you can be given spiritual food. I make a distinction between dreams in the usual sense that have a psychological meaning, and dreams that I call "experiences" because a different part of consciousness is present. "Dream experiences" are different from ordinary dreams because they go beyond the individual's mind to a greater source where wisdom is contacted and instruction is received. Dream experiences have a tremendous impact on how you live your life afterwards.

When you first have a small experience—an insight like a flash of awareness—if you invoke a feeling of gratitude, many more flashes of awareness will come. It is as if I ask you for a favor, and when you respond very nicely, I thank you sincerely. Then you will be willing to help me again. If your ego just brushes the experience off, it may not return. Treat your own Higher Self in the same way. Give it power to come into the foreground. It will exercise its power in a most beneficial way.

Dreams can prepare you for a little more, and then a little more. But if you do not pay attention to your insights, including your hunches, and if you take everything for granted, one of two things can happen: intuition may disappear entirely for the rest of your life, or you may experience a strong force from your Higher Self that pushes your objections and callousness aside and says, "Listen. Now *pay attention!"* Then you can have an extraordinary experience.

The following dream, "Solitary Confinement," was almost like a telepathic contact that gave me vital instructions for my spiritual development.

Solitary Confinement

I entered a big building, which I realized was a prison. People were sitting at long tables, very focused on what they had right in front of them, looking down, bent over. Then the prison warden asked me, "Would you like to go to the upper levels where the prisoners are in solitary confinement?"

"Yes," I said. Then I asked him, "Do these people know they are in prison?"

"No, and they are quite happy with what they are doing. They are captivated by it. That's all they focus on."

I felt very astonished at this. Is it possible that people are in prison and don't even know it? I could hardly get over it. Not only did they seem to be unaware of where they were, but they were also apparently happy.

We went up to another level, where the more dangerous prisoners were kept in solitary confinement. There was one man in particular whom I noticed in a cell like a small cage. On the wall was a very straight bed with a simple blanket where he was sitting in a perfect lotus posture with his eyes closed. I stood quietly and watched him. He looked peaceful. After a little while he opened his eyes, and I asked, "Do you know that you are in prison?" "Yes," he said.

"Do you have to work here?"

"A little."

"What else do you do?"

"I leave the prison. I go somewhere else."

"Where do you go?"

"To places of great knowledge. And because of this freedom I do not mind being here, as there is always time to do what is important after I have done what is requested of me." "But how do you get out?" The walls of the prison were bare concrete.

"Oh, I just sit here quietly and 'think' my way out," he explained to me. "The guard knows to some extent that he is in prison. All the others in the big hall down below don't know. But I can think my way out. I leave my body and come back without anyone knowing. Only in solitary confinement are we free." I was rather puzzled by that.

"Not even the warden knows of my freedom," he added.

I looked at the warden-guide. He seemed absent-minded. His face was somehow "clouded." I was speechless, amazed and shaken.

"Do you read books?" I asked when my voice came back. "Do you study metaphysical books?" He said he read a little and that there was some stimulation in books, but all that mattered was thinking through and thinking one's way out!

"Are there other prisoners in solitary confinement?"

"Yes," he nodded. "Some do the same. Some have not yet reached the same freedom."

I felt my mind working at tremendous speed. Finally I got hold of the thought that seemed to be paramount. Where was this prison? The world? The body? The mind? The ashram?

He smiled again. It put me at ease. "Ashram and world are the same. Therefore the prison is the body and the mind. It is good that you see the prison walls where they are. That is the first step to freedom."

He stretched out his hand to me. I took it with both of mine.

"Solitary confinement! Solitary confinement!" With those words I awoke.

I immediately understood that the ground floor of the prison represented ordinary life. Most people do not know they are in a prison. They are under the illusion that life is great and gives them what they want. When I first started asking people what the purpose of their life was, they would give me blank looks and say, "What a strange question! I have my family, my children, my work." They were prisoners who did not know that they were in prison—the prison of their ideas, the prison of their concepts, and especially the prison of their concept of what life was about. The dream assured me that there was no need to be concerned about those who did not yet know that they were in prison, because others, "the wardens," would take care of them.

Stimulation in small quantities—carefully selected books—seemed to be all right if thinking stayed the main work—thinking things through and thinking my way out. Thoughts have to be directed. I had recognized early in my life that undirected thoughts had a negative influence on my physical well-being and my psychic strength. I had noticed that ambitious businessmen, despite pressure from all sides, often seemed less tired than people who allowed their thoughts to roam, even if their bodies were quite relaxed.

"Only in solitary confinement are we free." Only in self-imposed solitary confinement can we think our way out of our prisons. Solitary confinement to most people is probably the worst condition imaginable, and those who have experienced it—people held hostage, for example—say they were afraid of losing their minds. But I knew that solitary confinement could have other possibilities.

Solitary confinement could mean being isolated from all influences that can manipulate the mind, being isolated from all influences from the senses. So when all these influences and manipulations are gone, an incredible power can be released that can work for the Divine and overcome many obstacles. To make contact with something else within ourselves, which we can call the Divine or the guru within, we need to confine ourselves to solitude, to quietness, to meditation. Then when the inner guru takes over, it can present new realities to us through dreams and experiences.

The prisoner in the dream experience had an incredible freedom. He would just sit, close his eyes and leave his body. He could go to places of great knowledge. Nobody knew he had gone. What was it then that leaves? The spiritual spark? If it could leave and go to another area or if it could offer help to others, then perhaps I, too, could do this if I put myself into the Light. I practiced this for years, saying, "This physical house is protected in the spiral of Light. Now something else—my soul or inner Light, the vortex of energy that we call 'consciousness'—can do the other work where the body cannot go." Eventually I received confirmation that this was indeed so.

I learned that consciousness does not have to take the body along. And the fact that when you "wake up," you find yourself in the chair where you were meditating or the bed where you were sleeping does not mean that you have to dismiss such an experience as a hallucination. If we sit outside and suddenly smell the perfume of flowers coming to us, we have not gone to the flower and the flower has not come to us. The perfume is invisible. We cannot see how it travels; but if we have a certain sensitivity, we can become aware of that perfume. It is similar with these experiences. It is the spark of life's essence that is able to move freely. What we bring along is that vortex of energy that is not necessarily visible to the senses.

Some time later the same dream experience recurred—the same prison, the same guard, the same prisoner in solitary confinement.

You Must Kill!

This time I asked him, "Would I have to *commit* something in order to be sentenced to solitary confinement?"

"Exactly," he responded.

"Why did you get solitary confinement?"

"I killed."

"Oh, my God!"

And he said, "One day you will have to kill."

"No, I can't do this. Do I *have* to kill?"

"Yes."

"There is no other way?"

"No."

Then he looked at me and asked, "Do you know *what* you have to kill?"

And in the dream I knew. I had to kill the part of my mind that constantly creates and produces desires.

I have to kill the scheming of the mind. How would I go about that? The answer was really in the Bhagavad Gita.[48] All the power of desires had to be brought together and focused entirely on the Divine. Then I had to accept that the Divine gives, the Divine takes away. I would not say, "Oh wonderful! I am so happy to have been given this or that!" or "How terrible! Look at all my losses!"

I had to find the place in the middle and be able to say: "I shall neither be overjoyed, nor will I cry. Some things are wonderful and I can appreciate them as long as I have them, but if the Divine wants them, I will give them back. Life is given, the opportunity to serve the Divine is given, and though my desire is great I will come home only when I have fulfilled my promise."

EXERCISES AND REFLECTIONS

1. You need to find time to extract yourself from daily life, to confineyourself to going within, to meditation. It is in solitude that the

opening happens. If I knock on your door long enough and intensely enough, you will open it. The guru within will not even keep you waiting that long.

In solitude, you can intensify your awareness in spiritual practices. Reflect on what each line of the Divine Light Mantra really means to you. Observe what actually happens when you chant a mantra. Become aware of the vibrations in the body and the effects of the vibrations of the mind.

2. Continue the practice of wrapping yourself in Light before you go to sleep,"protecting the house, the physical body."

chapter 27

SUBSTANTIATION OF SPIRITUAL DREAMS

We cannot always be sure when dreams come from a higher source, so we have to be cautious in our conclusions. If a dream is very positive it is easy to assume that it is a Divine message. But each of us has many voices—the inner voices of our personality aspects—and if you do not know all your personality aspects, it is not so easy to determine which voice is the Higher Self. Anxiety, jealousy, temptation, admiration—all have voices. Which is which? After many years of working with my dreams, I am still extremely careful because I know the tricks of the mind.

You will need to investigate how many voices you have. In this process it is important that you do not judge or blame yourself. Simply learn to distinguish between the voices of your different personality aspects. Then keep careful records of your dreams, write them down, and if you act on a dream that you think is from a higher source, find out if the results of your actions measure up to the dream. How does the dream influence your behavior? If the dream was empowered by the ego, you may feel compelled to assert yourself. But if the influence was from the Divine, you will function from true devotion, humility and sincerity. Do not ever assume that you "have arrived" and that you no longer need to work on yourself.

When you have a dream or visionary experience of the Divine, you need to know whether the mind has manufactured it or whether is a true experience. If you have a very elated feeling, and if you cannot reproduce the experience again by your own imagination, you have two clues. You can repeat experiences created by your own imagination, but the real experiences and that feeling of elation you cannot repeat. Yet, when the mind is in what I call the "twilight state," an in-between state where it is open and receptive but also suggestible, you still have to ask, "How do I know for sure?"

Ask whether the dream is spiritual, and then wait until you receive a confirmation or substantiation. Substantiation is not absolute proof—there is no absolute proof. Dreams cannot be repeated like scientific experiments. But if you receive something tangible related to the dream, you have evidence that is at least convincing to your own mind. You may dream that a particular gift is coming your way. Though you are not able to perceive the source of the gift, you may feel it is from a higher level. If you eventually receive that gift in waking life, the dream is substantiated and you have the best evidence that the mind did not create a fantasy out of its own tremendous need for survival. Once the survival level is left behind, dreams can be incredibly instructive—helping you to open the door to the Divine within, helping you to find the entrance to that Cathedral of Consciousness.

Not every dream needs to be substantiated, but enough do so that you can tell the difference between an intense dream that was empowered by the ego, and one that was truly influenced by the Divine. I wait and see. I have often been given pieces of jewelry, which I think of as "spiritual jewelry" because they served to confirm or verify certain dream experiences.

After I had returned to Canada from India, I was sending monthly reports to my Guru and asking for his advice, but I never received further instructions. At the time I wanted to know if I was doing things correctly, and when I did not receive an answer I became quite discouraged. But one night I had this dream.

The First To Come

A very blond child came to me with a whole handful of jewelry and said, "This is all waiting for you, and you will get these one by one." He held out a ring to me and said, "This will be the first to come."

I looked at the ring, and I felt partly surprised, partly overjoyed and partly shocked. The ring was in the design of a crusader's cross, and I had no desire to be either a crusader or a missionary. I did not think in terms of fulfilling my mission in life.

Some time later, under most unusual circumstances, a diamond ring set in the form of a crusader's cross was given to me. The experience assured me that signs confirming our progress on the spiritual path do come. The ring was a substantiation of the dream.

I never asked for a substantiation of the dream, but it happened. This and other substantiations confirmed the reality that otherwise would have been hard for me to accept—the kinds of dreams that seemed too good to be true. For me, having a material manifestation—something that remained visible— was enough evidence that these special dream experiences had an undeniable reality. We have already examined the power of wishful thinking and know that a desire, when combined with strong emotions, may eventually manifest. But some manifestations have little to do with the limited powers of our own minds.

To show you what I mean, I will give you a detailed example of a dream experience and how it was substantiated.

The Two Chariots

I cannot describe the place I'm at, but several crates are being delivered to me. The first crate opens itself somehow to reveal a beautiful golden chariot. Fantastic! I am tremendously impressed by it and very excited. At the same time, I am aware of the dream's importance and feel a sense of urgency to remember it and write it down.

The entire chariot is pure gold and emerges from the crate all in one piece. I run my fingers along the design on the side. It is like a piece of jewelry—extraordinary, beautiful—reflecting the light with a soft glow. Then I see another person, who gestures for me to come to the other side of the chariot. As I walk around it I see flashes of blue light, and there, on the back of one of the seats I see, written in dazzling blue sapphires, R-A-D-H-A. The second seat is unmarked. I am stunned. I think, "It could only be Lord Krishna's chariot!"

At this point, my feeling of urgency wakes me, and I repeat the dream to myself with a feeling of surprise and tremendous joy, realizing that the Divine will not let me down. Despite the many problems over the years, the Divine will always keep its promise—this is the message. After I write down the dream, I remember the other crates and feel I must find out what they contain. Very brief images of Radha and Krishna flit through my mind as I lie down again. Then the full scene reappears, without losing any detail.

The golden chariot is still there for me to see. And now I am given help in opening the other crates. I see pieces of beautifully carved sandalwood, which I realize will form another chariot —a bigger one—when the pieces are all put together. There are many pieces and it may take quite some time to fit them all together so that the chariot can be used. The carvings are of the finest quality, very intricate and delicate.

I have the feeling, "These carvings are too exquisite to be burned." I also have the thought, "But there are no horses. The chariot is Krishna's chariot; and there is my name, RADHA, but there are no horses." Then a voice says, "The horses will be here when the time comes."

When I wake up again, a question appears in my mind: "When will I ride in the golden chariot, and when will I ride in the wooden carved one?" The golden chariot must be the vehicle of my Higher Self, to carry it home. The wooden chariot is, perhaps, the body. One day it will burn, because I have always wanted my body to be cremated. The body will be taken in a vehicle to the crematorium long after the golden chariot has disappeared with the essence of Radha.

Yes, I could understand that. The body is a vehicle. Sylvia is a vehicle for that particular ray of Light called Radha.[49] That the chariot has to be put together was true, because my body had suffered and needed to heal. The various parts of my body had to function better so the body could work better as a whole. But I felt it was also quite possible that the pieces of the chariot could refer to my notes and writings, those insights and inspirations that I had jotted down over the years in the hope that I would have time to put them together one day. Although the dream announced that the golden chariot was here, it also said the wooden chariot still has to be assembled. This made me realize that I might have to resign myself to living longer, until the job was done.

Still, the message of the dream was so extraordinary, so promising. I wanted to be sure that I was not tricking myself by strong, wishful thinking—even if it came from my heart—so I said to myself, "This dream seems too good to be true. I can hardly believe it. The golden chariot is like a piece of jewelry. If I ever see a piece of jewelry like this chariot, then I will really accept the dream as a message from the Divine." But, I thought, "Who would ever make a piece of jewelry in the shape of a chariot, and if somebody did make it, who would wear it?"

Some years earlier, a student of mine had been talking to me about a career change. We had tossed around all kinds of ideas, and he had talked about his interests and mentioned that somebody in his family was in the jewelry business, which quite intrigued him. One day I was at an antique store and I happened to see a pamphlet on courses offered in gemology, so I picked one up and gave it to him. He was delighted, and immediately started taking courses in antique jewelry.

He went really enthusiastically into his research. He talked to other people in the business, took courses in both business and gems, bought a number of books on diamonds and semi-precious stones and equipment, and went to exhibits. He was very interested and loved to talk about it. One weekend, he went to a wonderful exhibition of antique jewelry. At the close of the exhibition he was trying to decide whether or not to pick up one of their catalogues for an auction being held in Toronto. The catalogues were quite expensive and he would be unable to attend the auction, so in some ways it did not make sense. But he thought it over, and when he saw that the one in front of him was the last one, he decided to purchase it.

When he showed me the catalogue, he said, "This is all antique jewelry, and I'll bet I know your taste so well that I could point out exactly what you would like." So we sat together and enjoyed leafing through the book.

And suddenly—there it was! A tiny, exquisitely crafted gold brooch in the form of a chariot. I was so enchanted by it that my friend immediately asked if he could give it to me as a gift, and though the auction was in Toronto and he was on the West Coast, he managed to put in his bid and successfully purchase this very special piece.

He phoned me to say, "Your golden chariot is on the way." This time the chariot arrived not in a crate, but in a tiny parcel.

What could I do now? Could I say my dream was a fantasy? A desire? Only my imagination? No. But what *must* I say? That my obligation to Krishna should be a thousandfold more, because the symbol was a tangible confirmation of the dream's reality.

By the way, shortly after this, my friend completely lost interest in the jewelry business. In fact, when I told him the whole story, he laughingly said that the Divine had used him for its own ends.

This kind of substantiation happened not just with this one piece of jewelry, but with many pieces—so many that the first dream of the little boy showing me the jewelry and saying I would receive each piece, one by one, has been realized.

I wonder if the people who have given me these lovely gifts realize that they have been messengers of the Divine. For me the gifts were especially precious because they had come from friends who were attracted to the teachings and understood what I was doing. If these people remember having been the messengers of the Divine, perhaps that thought will give them enough support in their own struggles that they, in turn, can inspire others.

When you have concrete evidence that your dream has a level of reality beyond the psychological, you can ask yourself, "What was different about this dream? How did I feel? How did the dream come about?" When you recognize the pattern, you can wait for its recurrence. After you have had a number of similar experiences and they have been substantiated, you really know that you can receive messages from the Divine through your dreams.

But the more you try to understand before you experience, the less you will ever truly experience. You can only experience first and then try to explain it later, and most of the time even that explanation does not work. Whatever comes from the Divine should be received as a gift. I have not tried to use my intellect to find a reason why it has come—that would be like taking the gift apart to see how good it is on the inside. It is better to allow feelings of gratitude and awe to well up for what the Divine is and gives than to want an explanation.

There will come a time when we no longer need any confirmations, when we recognize and trust the Divine messages. But it is very good not to stop questioning too soon. Because again and again I have seen how tricky the mind can be and how it can create so much out of a survival need.

It has become perfectly clear to me that when we pick up the clues and put them all together, we will find quite a number of messages from the Divine. We are never really left without confirmations if we are just more attentive and if we do not take any gift for granted.

EXERCISES AND REFLECTIONS

1. The practice of returning to a particular dream to carry the dream intowaking consciousness is a very important one. Do you ever have dreams where you dream a bit, wake up, and then go back and continue the dream? It is like reading a book. You lay the book aside and when you come back to it, you go over the last paragraph you read and then continue from there.

2. Get to know your personality aspects and their different voices. You canobserve them in your everyday interactions. Make a list of them. You can even give them names. Become familiar enough with them that you can distinguish which personality aspects speak in the dream.

3. If you have a dream that you think is from a higher source, observe howthe dream influences your behavior. Dream experiences have a dramatic impact on your life. See also if the dream is substantiated in the particular way in which you can recognize and accept it.

chapter 28

THE PROMISE: MYSTICAL UNION

The moments when we rise above the whole bundle of our personalities and really function through our essence are extremely rare. It is a rare moment when we really act out of love for the Divine. Such moments express what I call "a love affair with the Divine." In dreams and mythology this love between the devotee and the Divine is often represented by a marriage or union. There is nothing that compares to it. Through very special, inspiring dreams we can be lifted out of ourselves to experience this Divine Love. These special dream experiences are what some people may call "visions" or "spiritual experiences." They are really meditative experiences that occur in a state when the conscious mind is not active.

Perhaps there truly is no other love than Divine Love. The human love we seek is an illusion—the fulfillment of the concept that each one of us has about love. But the Divine almost constantly has to overlook all our faults, mistakes, shortcomings, broken promises, broken intentions and human weaknesses. We can be very scattered in our approach to the Divine or very rigid. If we are regular and persistent in our practices, we can become routine and lose depth, yet if we do not persist and do not pursue our goal, our intentions are like sparks flashing here and there, coming to nothing. Yet still Divine Love is there.

We cannot love the Divine in the same way that we love an object or another person. With the Divine you feel happy that after all you have been through, you have finally made your way back again. Certainly you are aware of how long you have been away—the time of separation—and you feel joyfully ecstatic to be back.

The only permanent love is love from the Divine—even when you do not recognize it, even when you feel separated. As long as you do not turn away, the Divine is facing you all the time. The Divine does not turn away. The sun does not disappear from the sky when it is covered by clouds. Divine Light is covered only by the clouds of your own thinking and your own emotions, and when the Light breaks through the clouds it is like consciousness breaking through to another dimension.

I would not claim even today to know what love is. Is a powerful commitment love itself? That could be. If commitment to the Divine is an expression of love for the Divine, then the protection from the Divine is an expression of love from the Divine. I can see the interdependence: The human depends on the Divine and yet the Divine also depends on the human form, the human voice and human love to convey and manifest Divine Love.

I have found that the divinity within ourselves will respond to what we need on the human level because that human aspect also needs nourishment. The obstacle is often that we feel we are too bad or too sinful to accept our own divinity, and if we do accept the Divine within, it is almost dangerous to acknowledge it to anybody else because it will be interpreted as ego. We have to watch, too, that our own human nature does not try to destroy out of jealousy whatever the Divine produces or the emerging Divine spark. Doubts can be a kind of attack, a war that the mind has with our own Divine nature.

When I needed help to keep me going spiritually, I had a series of dreams. These experiences, which were more than dreams, were needed to balance the challenges I was facing in my daily life. This series came cloaked in Christian symbolism, probably influenced by my retreat and meditation on the book of Revelation and its relation to the Kundalini system. For many years of my life the Pope had appeared in books and magazines as a symbol of the Divine. The Pope is said to walk in the shoes of Peter and to be the representative of Jesus on Earth. I probably accepted this at one time and incorporated it into my personal symbolism.

The dream series that follows is an example of consciousness breaking through to another dimension. Recalling such significant dreams is extremely important, even though memory is not the actual experience. If I eat a piece of fruit or drink a glass of wine, later I can only remember the experience; that remembering is not the experience itself. What is stirred in the memory is the effect, the reflection, the echo, of what the actual experience of eating the fruit or drinking the wine created in me.

If I awaken the memory of remarkable dreams and experiences by going through my diary, excerpting these special events and reflecting on them, I can bring back to life that which responded in me at the time. Naturally, with dream experiences and experiences of the Light, the effect is much greater than the memory of a pleasant taste on the tongue.

Another way to increase your ability to receive spiritual dreams is to say thank you to your Higher Self. Give that recognition to the source of the dream. Do not take its gifts for granted. I understood from the beginning that we cannot take even the most beautiful insight, dream, inspiration or vision to mean that now we can take our spiritual evolution for granted, without making any further efforts. At no point in life, and probably not in the afterlife either, can we take anything for granted. That is probably the greatest mistake we can make—taking each other for granted and taking the Divine for granted.

Receiving the Mantle

I find myself in a church of exquisite beauty. A very special service is going on, and I wonder what the meaning of this service is. There are a great number of dignitaries and only a few ordinary people like myself. I am in the back of the big room, but somehow I can still see everything quite well. I am not entirely unfamiliar with the service in a Catholic Church, but this Mass is all in Latin, which I do not understand, so I follow only what I recognize: the offerings.

Then each of these great men in their beautiful robes is handed a piece of paper on which they quickly write something. The papers are then collected in a large bowl before the altar. One priest leads a prayer and all chant a hymn. The same priest takes three papers from the bowl. Then an official, wearing a red robe with a white lace collar, comes over to me.

I feel terribly embarrassed. "Gosh, I should not be here. I am discovered at their very special service. Somebody will get in trouble for having overlooked the presence of a stranger." The priest asks me to step forward to receive my mantle. I don't know what to do.

I whisper, "But it is all a mistake. I should not be here. I am sorry to disturb you. I assure you, I did not mean to."

He looks at me sternly, saying, "Will you please come to the altar to receive your mantle. It is the Lord's decision."

So I get up and follow him, hoping for the best. The mantle is a pearl gray color and I am given a black top hat to put on. Then I am told I have fifteen minutes before my speech. I go back to my place. I can't think. My mind rattles like an old car motor, the wheels turn wildly. When I discover

that all eyes are on me, I decide to go to the washroom to be alone and think clearly for a few minutes about my speech. I am sure God will help me.

When I am in the washroom, I hear someone opening the door behind me. I step into the little booth but I can't close the door because there is nothing to close it with. The person passes by. "Goodness, it is the Pope! He sees me. Am I in the men's room? Well, I'll have to make the best of it." I walk out, bowing reverently to him and trying to assume the best attitude I can— heart, mind and soul. I will just explain to him that I am not Catholic.

But he doesn't let me. Instead, he takes my arm and firmly motions me out and back to the big church room. As we walk up the steps, I dare to interrupt him with a very personal remark. I say, "I know you are the Pope, but I don't even know how to address you. See! You have the wrong person."

"I am called the Holy Father, you see, and you will be given your name as soon as we arrive," he replies. He caresses my arm with gentleness, and looks at me with a deep and great expression of love.

It takes my last scrap of courage to say, "Holy Father, I am not a Catholic, don't you understand? I intruded into your church. You selected me in all ignorance of my status as a stranger. I am terribly sorry to cause you this inconvenience."

"Never mind about being a stranger. We, the holy Church and I and its Founder—Jesus' follower"—he points to a figure of Jesus—"believe in this ceremony, and that God alone makes this decision. Don't worry about not being Catholic. We will see to that." A moment of silence. "I, myself, shall baptize you. I, myself, shall receive you into His arms. Now let us go."

So we go. We come to the church door. I try to open it for the Holy Father but he doesn't let me. "Not today," he whispers as he opens the door. All present look at us. They rise. The Pope walks to the altar. I stay behind, waiting his bidding. Someone offers me his chair. I sit down. A lovely high-sounding bell rings, like crystal when tapped with a silver spoon. I know my time has come.

My heart beats furiously. I keep walking, reach the chair of the Pope, and kneel down. A choir starts singing. But I can clearly hear the Pope saying, while laying his hands on my head: "Repeat: 'I am of lowly birth, lowly action, lowly speech. But by Thy grace I shall now lay all that I am at Thy feet. I have now received your mercy. I have received a new coat and a new name. I shall do all work in His name with His power.'" I feel so shaken, I can hardly keep on my knees.

"Open your mouth," the Pope says. I do. He places the host into it and puts a glass of red wine on my lips.

The coolness of the glass is still with me.

I hear someone coming. Oh, they are coming to the Prayer Room. Good—then I am behind this great altar in the church. I am now with the Pope. Oh no, it's Kootenay Bay. [50]

Someone is coming to sing mantras. Wonderful. It's time, then, to get up. What a dream. My heart is still beating. My body feels sweaty. But I have to write down the dream first. I will feel better.

Now that the dream is on paper, my mind runs wild again. Previous dreams rush into my mind—the Upper Room where someone will meet me, my childhood experience playing with little angels, the Ave Maria. Then I begin to think, "But I have become a sanyasin, why would I dream in Christian symbolism?" Other experiences with the Buddha, with Divine Mother, with Krishna rush into my mind. How does this all fit together? A memory arises of one of the more advanced Kundalini exercises—visualizing the lotus at the base of the spine, first closed and then slowly opening. In the center of the lotus is a diamond of many facets. Divine power has many facets. It will use whatever shape, form and color to communicate itself. God is one; Divine names are many.

With this thought I enter a peaceful meditation.

A few nights later, I had the following dream.

In the Garden

I am in a beautiful garden where many different types of flowers are in full bloom. As I walk along a sunlit path, I meet the Pope again. We walk together, hand in hand, and talk in a very friendly way about great and wonderful teachings. He explains many things to me. I am amazed at his wisdom and feel extremely happy—a happiness that I had never dreamed was possible. Every now and then I remember that the Pope walks in the shoes of Jesus, and I cannot wonder enough about how privileged I am to be with him. I silently promise myself to stay on this Path of Light, which is like a taste of heaven.

When I look around at the amazing variety of flowers and trees, it becomes even clearer to me that while God is one and without gender, the same creative force has expressed itself in an incredible multitude of ways—too vast ever to be grasped by the limitations of a human mind.

If we recognize the preciousness and the many facets in the many religions, if we stay focused on the beauty, the Light and the wisdom that all religions have in common, then we can truly be a family of the Divine, and see ourselves as the creation of this Divine Cosmic Energy.

The third dream in this continuing series occurred several nights later.

The Wedding Awaits

I hear one of the young disciples calling outside my cabin, "Swamijiiii," several times. And as he comes closer his voice sounds louder. Then with a big bang he opens the door, still calling so loudly that it feels as if the roof will come down, "Swamijiiii!" "What is it?" I ask him.

"They are all waiting for you. Hurry. Hurry. The Wedding. The Pope is already there!" Suddenly he looks at me and says, "Oh, that is beautiful! How beautiful, Swamiji! You must wear this always."

Now I look at myself and am just as surprised as he is. My body is transparent Light—I have no real dress but no real body, either. I am in a daze and go out and up the hill where the Cathedral is. The doors are wide open, and as I approach I hear lovely music—like organ music and like a choir of angels chanting.

Then I stand at the door. The sight is so overpowering I cannot move—not one single step. The big room where I had received my mantle is already of such exquisite beauty, there are just no words to

describe it. I see the Pope sitting on a throne in fantastic splendor—an unthinkable splendor, and yet here it is. I am so overwhelmed, almost paralyzed, that I go to the lake, sit down and cry in sheer joy.

It is the Wedding—the Union between the Divine and me—so unthinkable and yet true. It seems too much to accept. I feel I've had my reward already, just knowing, even if the doors are closed again. If I walk up now to enter, the opportunity alone—my God, oh my God—what great wonders . . .

The first dream with the Pope: meeting the soul or Higher Self. The second dream with the Pope in the beautiful gardens: getting last instructions. Now comes the long-awaited Wedding—the Union— and a new view—seeing things in their true perspective. This is a new experience of humility of quite an unknown quality. It is a joy at the same time. Even this glimpse of the Reality—the only one there is—is enough. This experience is an incentive. It will be the source of strength for whatever may come. The stage for the last drama is already set. It is now up to me to do the rest.

In this final dream I had to make a decision. Should I stay here or should I go now? I knew if I entered the Cathedral, that would be the end of my life. In the dream I went to the lake to reflect. When a certain state of Realization is reached, the body falls away between nine and twenty-one days afterwards, and it will only stay on longer if you have a particular job to do. I felt a temptation to go, but I knew I had to keep my promise.

Out of this experience I received a powerful insight into the different temptations of the Buddha and Jesus. Jesus' temptation was the world, so he overcame it by teaching for only three years. The Buddha's temptation was what we call "Heaven," and he overcame this by staying on Earth to help people. The biggest difficulty for me after these dreams was to keep working and functioning on the ordinary three-dimensional level. I became so transparent and sensitive that life around me was almost unbearable. I would think, "I am not waiting for anything, I am not looking for anything, I have no unfulfilled desires. Why don't I go?"

I understood that the spiritual world is one world, but that does not mean that everything in the physical world is influenced in the way we would hope or expect. On Earth the river flows downward; it is only in heaven where the river can flow upward. The mystical tree is rooted in heaven, where it can get nourishment and then grow toward the Earth. So even if we are rooted in heaven, we still have to grow toward the Earth—nobody asks if we want to.

When life does not make sense, it is very hard to stay involved. It is very hard to keep doing something that does not make sense. There was a temptation to enter the Cathedral, it is true. But a broken promise would have meant I had let the Divine down. Clearly the Divine has guided every single step of my life up to this point, and will do so in the future. I must keep my commitment.

chapter 29

JOURNEY TO THE LIGHT

I am not sure if you can develop an intense desire for the Light. Often we cannot even develop a love affair with another person, and a love affair with the Divine is much more difficult to attain. Through our experiences in life we have to reach the point of intensely wanting to know, wanting to understand and wanting to move on. Think how much more difficult it is for premature babies to survive than babies delivered when their time is due.

Each of us has to go through the process of growing to maturity.

The following dream was an inspiration, a dream that needed little interpretation or commentary. One thing it made clear is that the spiritual journey takes a long time. We have to consider that even a temple or cathedral is often not completed in the same century it was started. In the same way the Cathedral of Consciousness also takes time to complete. Inspiration can be a sustaining energy, but it does not mean you can lessen your efforts.

Whatever we gain by our own efforts to come closer to the Divine is never lost. And whenever we do make contact, we can never forget. The memory is too overpowering. The memory is too sweet. You want it again, so you pull yourself together and say, "I will give it another try," until you finally get there. It is just like exercising muscles, except in this case, it is exercising the mind to overcome obstacles and resistance. People often find it difficult to attain a spiritual state because they resist. Resisting the Divine is also the source of depressions and negative moods. You know that the Divine is standing behind the door, but you do not want to open it. You wonder fearfully, "What is She going to ask?" "What is He going to demand?" And yet you want . . . and you don't want, you want and you don't want. Because you cannot make up your mind, you resist. Nobody holds you back except yourself.

In the dream I am presented with a choice: I can continue to go through the swamp and probably eventually sink into it, disappear and find my spiritual death; or I can enter the stream, which has a more solid base. The swamp to me is life without purpose. Some people say they want spiritual life but they still want to keep their business interests, their family interests and their control over future plans; then they get lost in the morass of life itself. But walking against the current demands tremendous effort. Living opposed to the normal concepts of life, which I have done, does require effort. Stones in the water are certainly not a soft cushion or carpet for the feet. So if you want to find out what it really means to live a spiritual life, you have to be prepared to go through the trials.

It is not a comfortable journey.

Journey to the Light

I am crossing some marshlands, jumping from one wooden board to another with a small bundle of my possessions. (Someone must have placed the planks here and there along the way.) Then I see a small stream with stones on the bottom, which looks like a firmer, safer base than the marshy morass. Although I have never walked with bare feet very much, I take off my shoes and enter the stream. The water is knee deep and the ground proves to be firm, as I had hoped. But I realize that it is not so easy to walk against the water.

I know that my destination is another shore, and that there will be a house there, and that I am expected. The stream gradually becomes a river, and then widens almost to the size of an ocean so vast that the opposite shore is now invisible. But I just know I have to make it there. I have no choice. I tie my bundle to the top of my head and decide to swim—it is the only solution, since the water has become too deep to walk through. I am not a very good swimmer so I think things through first. I decide to breathe regularly, take slow big strokes, and not hurry, in order to maintain my strength to the very last moment. I am convinced that I will be able to make it.

For some time I can see a dim little light, which I believe comes from "that" house. But then it, too, disappears and I start to get worried about how I will stay on course. Then I become aware that the water has a warm stream, which seems to go straight ahead. I try to keep to this warmer stream. My feet seem especially sensitive to recognizing the difference in temperature while swimming.

Finally I reach the shore. Again I see the little light more clearly, but I am surprised that it still seems far away. At first I think of taking a rest, but then, looking again at the light, I decide to keep going and get it over with. Moving ahead seems a little easier now. The field between the shore and the house is a soft kind of grass. But still I cannot seem to cover the ground as quickly as I thought, and the distance seems greater than I had anticipated.

At last I reach the house, only to face one more obstacle—there is no door. Yet I know, very definitely, that I am at the right place. Above the ground are large windows. I see there is no other way in but to climb up. Even though I do not like climbing and it looks as if it will be difficult to hold on and balance myself, there is no choice. I walk around the house. Light floods from the windows and almost blinds me, but I know I have to climb up anyway. I cannot wait here forever, so near my goal.

The building is solid stone. I get a grip with just my fingertips and toes, and inch my way up. It is a terrible struggle. At the last moment, just when I think I can't make it, my hand reaches the windowsill, and the window opens from the inside. I am pulled into the room. When I am inside I look at my helper with great relief, knowing that now it is all over!

The helper is a being of such indescribable beauty that I fall to the floor and just stare. That is all I feel capable of.

This wonderful being—I do not know if it is an angel or a bodhisattva—beaming with great joy, says, "All people must come sooner or later. All must find their way."

The helper directs me to look out the window. I see many, many little dots of light like glowworms or fireflies.

I say, "But when I was swimming and walking here, I did not see any of these. I would have been happy if I had. It was very dark, and I was absolutely alone."

"They feel alone, too. Utterly alone. It cannot be otherwise. But would you like to help them, now that you are here?"

"Me? I can't do anything!"

"You can say a prayer, can you not?"

I agree. When I look out the window, suddenly I feel again the strain and anxiety I had felt along the way, and a wave of compassion overcomes me.

"Dear Lord, let none get lost," is all I can manage. The prayer seems to come from my heart rather than from my mouth. In fact, I am aware of how insufficient, meaningless and empty words are—how sentimental.

When this servant of the Light motions me to turn around and sit down, I see that what had appeared to be a small house is really an enormous palace, extraordinarily beautiful and bright. More light floods through a sliding door, and then I hear indescribable music, unlike anything I have ever heard, like big choirs, from nowhere and everywhere. This music has a tremendous impact on me. This "Choir of Souls," I call it for lack of words, touches me to the core and I feel overawed.

The central thought in the dream is that I must reach my destination. I must arrive at Cosmic Consciousness, at the Divine, however dim or vague my ideas about it. "I just must" has so far truly kept me going, and the dream shows me it will continue to do so until all is done. The one thing that stays permanent throughout is my attraction to the Light. It is the propelling force that keeps me moving on. I never consider giving up.

Crossing the stream would have been very easy, but continuing right to the end—from the very narrow stream to the point where the river merges into the ocean, and then crossing to "the other shore"—that is a different challenge. The warm stream on the feet told me that as long as I stay in touch with my enthusiasm and intuition, I will keep going in the right direction. But the moment I experiment or try something easier, I may end up off course; I may literally cool off and let the direction go.

I am being led into the room where the voices of many are heard chanting the Divine glories. In the scriptures it says some will be carried to the heavens to do just that. Others are like bodhisattvas, who offer to come back to help further the Divine work.

This dream showed me that the higher mind is quite capable of perceiving other dimensions, but that the message has to be passed along in a way that the ordinary mind can understand; otherwise the meaning will remain concealed. Here was the map for my journey to the Light.

The dream's message is clear: if you persist, you will get there.

www.ingramcontent.com/pod-product-compliance
Lightning Source LLC
LaVergne TN
LVHW091317150826
845673LV00006B/1685
* 9 7 9 8 7 6 7 6 1 7 2 5 8 *